— THE OFFICIAL —
JOHN WAYNE
—HANDY BOOK OF—
BUSHCRAFT

ESSENTIAL TIPS AND TECHNIQUES FOR SURVIVING IN THE WILD

BILLY JENSEN, GREEN BERET (RET.)
AND CHECK FREEDMAN

INTRODUCTION

 ELF-SUFFICIENCY means different things to different people. For some, this notion is tied to the distant past, when man was responsible for building a fire no matter the weather, foraging for food no matter the season and fighting off danger no matter its form. But for many, these abilities remain just as relevant today.

Luckily, we have a timeless role model to cut through the confusion and show us what true self-sufficiency, and the rugged individuality that defines it, looks like—John Wayne. Duke, idolized as the epitome of grit for generations, could make his own fish hooks in the morning, reel in an impressive catch in the afternoon and prepare it for dinner over a whole log fire he built himself all before sundown. And, with a little elbow grease and the aid of this book, so can you.

Inspired by John Wayne's incomparable independence and informed by legitimate Green Beret training, this book has instructions and advice for performing more than 100 skills every individual should know before venturing out on the big trail. Whether you need to make your own knife, build a snow cave or navigate an erupting volcano, these techniques will help prepare you for the myriad challenges Mother Nature might throw your way. You may not be John Wayne by the time you turn the last page, but you'll be the next best thing: a self-sufficient survivor.

In 1968, John Wayne directed and starred in *The Green Berets*, a cinematic salute to the U.S. troops fighting overseas in the Vietnam War. The film was inspired by Robin Moore's 1965 novel of the same name, which detailed the author's experiences with Special Forces in Vietnam, as well as Duke's experience visiting troops in the summer of 1966 as part of a tour organized by the USO's Hollywood Overseas Committee. In recognition of his efforts, John Wayne was made an honorary Green Beret, and he remains one of the few in Hollywood history to hold that honor.

CONTENTS

CONSTRUCTING SHELTER

MASTERING YOUR SURROUNDINGS

FIRST AID

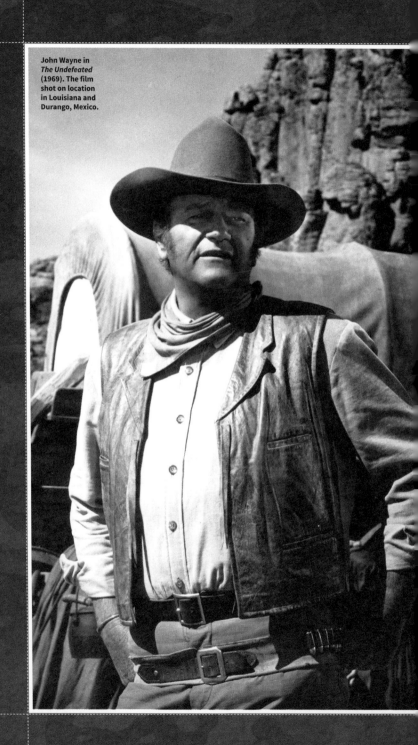

John Wayne in *The Undefeated* (1969). The film shot on location in Louisiana and Durango, Mexico.

ESSENTIAL TOOLS & SYSTEMS

LEARNING TO MAKE
AND USE THESE TOOLS
WILL SET YOU UP FOR
SUCCESS IN THE WILD.

HOW TO
MAKE A KNIFE

NIVES ARE among the most valuable tools you can have in the wild. If you ever find yourself in need, knowing how to make one can mean the difference between life and death. Here's how to do it.

You will need:
- Pine pitch (see note below)
- A stone (flint, shale, basalt, obsidian or chert)
- An animal horn, antler or a piece of wood (for the handle)
- Deer sinew, rawhide, gut or fibrous plants (for lashings)
- Sand
- A small round rock
- Fire

You'll also need sandstone, granite or any other round stone that will not break when you strike with it. A good place to look for round stones is in a river or creek bed.

NOTE Pine pitch is the same as pine sap. It is naturally occurring, and you can find it running down pine trees, in pine cones, in cut pine wood or by tapping a pine tree to allow it to run out.

1. Make a fire (see pgs. 102-137) and melt your pine pitch. Once it is melted, add ashes from your fire, one part ashes to three parts melted pitch. Mix them together and you have hot glue. Set that aside.

2. From a seated position, hold the round rock in your dominant hand, then hold the stone in your non-dominant hand and brace your hand on the thigh of your non-dominant leg. Strike the stone in small, sharp strikes away from you. You will chip pieces off. Make sure to take your time and pay attention to detail. You need to create a point, but be sure not to make it too thin. It's up to you to decide what size and shape to make your blade based on the size and thickness of your original piece of stone. You can alternate between striking the surface to chip pieces off and rubbing the newly created sharp edges to smooth them down.

3. If you are using cedar wood for your handle, strip the bark off and peel away every fiber that stands out and could produce splinters. You can rub the stripped wood smooth with your stone. Cut a notch in the center of one end of your handle just big enough to insert the blade, making sure the fit is snug and deep. Dip the base of your blade in the pine pitch glue and fit it down into the notch of the handle. Take your lashing material and wrap it snugly around the place where the blade and the handle meet. Be generous with your wraps.

4. Brush your pine pitch glue over the lashing and allow it to cool and harden. Remember to protect your blade as you carry it. Be sure not to drop it or jam it into anything—it is breakable if used incorrectly. This knife will not be for prying or twisting, but for stabbing and slicing with the tip.

NOTE Do not heat the river rocks in or near your fire. Because of the temperature differential, they may explode and throw dangerous shrapnel.

2   3   4

HOW TO
MAKE A SPEAR

PEARS ARE among the oldest tools made by humans, and they continue to be one of the most versatile. They can be used for hiking stabilization, reaching, hunting, fishing and many more applications. Here's how you can craft three versions of field expedient spears.

You will need:
- A straight shafted piece of wood or bamboo a foot taller than you
- A fixed-blade knife or a hatchet
- Deer sinew, rawhide, gut or fibrous plants (for lashings)
- Pine pitch (optional)
- A stone which can be flaked or chipped or a naturally pointy rock
- A fist-sized rock
- Two small sticks approximately 4 to 6 inches long and ¼-inch thick
- Fire

You want the shaft to be taller than you so that if you trip while running with the spear, you cannot impale yourself. Bamboo is ideal, but any sturdy tree limb can do the job. It needs to be easily handled so consider weight when you select your shaft. It must have enough weight to be thrown with force but not so much that carrying or using it tires you out.

1. To make a simple spear, simply strip the shaft of its bark. Use your knife to shave one end into a point and harden the point briefly over a fire. Jackpot. You have a spear.

2. To make a fishing spear, split the tip of the spear in two

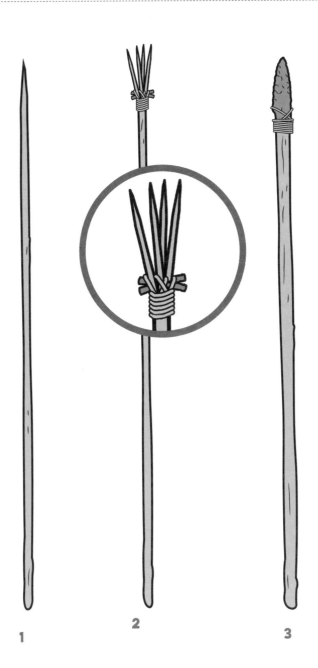

1

2

3

MAKE A SPEAR *continued*

directions: north/south and east/west. This should result
in four prongs. Each split should be about 6 inches deep.
Be careful not to allow any of the sections to peel off.
Wedge one small stick into one of the splits (north/south),
perpendicular to the spear. Wedge the other small stick
crosswise to the first one (east/west), also perpendicular
to the spear. Now you have a fishing spear that can both
impale the fish as well as grab it and bring it to the surface.

3. To make a complex spear, set your knife or hatchet blade
in the end of the shaft as a wedge and use your fist-sized
rock as a hammer. Slowly drive the knife into the spear
with the rock, splitting the end in two halves about 12
inches deep. If you are worried about the two halves
coming apart, you can tie your leather lashings or sinew
onto the shaft exactly where you want the bottom of the
split to be, making sure they are snug enough to hold
the wood together as you split the top. Take your pointy
rock or flaked/chipped stone and wedge it down deeply
between the two halves. Leave enough of the tip sticking
out to be an effective impaling device. Use your sinew,
rawhide, gut or fibrous plants to securely bind the shaft
of the spear around the spear head. If you would like,
you can also add pine pitch here to reinforce the binding,
though it is not necessary. This spear will be the hardest to
use because of the weight on one end.

To use any of these spears, hold in your dominant hand with
your palm up and find the point where the spear balances
in your hand. This place will be your grip. To aim, raise your
non-dominant arm straight out in front of you and point. As
you aim, hold the spear by its grip, raise it above your head,
take a lunging step forward with your non-dominant foot
and hurtle the spear into your target using your body weight.

John Wayne in
Allegheny Uprising
(1939). The film's
working titles were
Pennsylvania Uprising,
The First Rebel and
Allegheny Frontier.

HOW TO
MAKE A BOW
AND ARROWS

 ONG AGO, primitive man looked hungrily at some wild game in the distance and thought, "Gee, I'd really like to kill that animal but it's all the way over there!" And just like that, the bow and arrow was born. Here's how to craft your own.

You will need:
- A green and flexible sapling, about as wide as your hand and greater than 5 feet tall
- A green stick about 3 feet long and $\frac{1}{3}$-inch wide
- A fixed-blade knife
- A couple of feathers
- Pine pitch glue (see pg. 8)
- A generous amount of wide-leafed or fibrous plants that can be woven into a cord
- A fist-sized rock
- Fire

1. Fell your sapling and cut it into a 5-foot long section. Using your knife as a wedge and a rock to hammer the knife, split the sapling down about halfway. Repeat this at the other end of the sapling, leaving about 6 inches at the center for the handle. Shave the rest of the bow down until it's flat on both sides, resilient enough to spring back when bent and strong enough not to break. About an inch or two in from each end of the bow, cut a small notch on both shoulders for the string. Rub the wood smooth with your rock to prevent splinters.

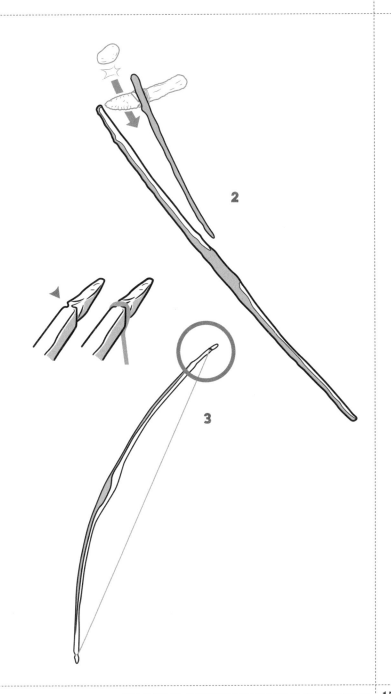

2

3

MAKE A BOW AND ARROWS *continued*

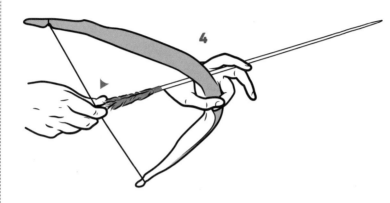

2. Take your stick and shave off the bark. Shave one end into a sharp point and harden the point over a fire. Using the pine pitch glue, attach two 2-inch feathers for fletching on opposite sides of the arrow near the blunt end and let it dry.

3. Peel the plant leaves into strips and rub the fibers between your fingers as they thin and stretch. Braid them together for strength, adding additional pieces of fiber as you braid to add length. This will form a rope for your string. Make a small loop in each end and place one into the two notches on one end of the bow. Bending the bow to fit the string, fit the other loop into the notches on the other end. The string should be taut and the bow nicely bent.

4. Cut a small notch in the blunt end of your arrow and fit it to your string. Holding the bow by the thick handle in the center, aim it at a target, pull the arrow back and release. Nice shot, pilgrim.

John Wayne in
The Conqueror (1956).
The film shot on
location in the Escalante
Desert region of
southern Utah.

HOW TO MAKE A STONE SLING

UST AS JOHN WAYNE honed his iconic persona for the big screen, the bulk of your time with this tool will be spent perfecting your technique. The stone sling or "slingshot" is an incredibly simple tool you can make quickly in a pinch. For an idea of how effective it can be, this is believed to be the same style of sling David used to kill Goliath in the Bible. Sometimes the old ways are still the best.

You will need:
- A small piece of hide
- Enough fibrous plants to braid into a rope about 4 feet long
- Small, smooth rocks
- A cutting device, such as a knife or a sharp rock
- A pencil-sized stick or an awl
- Fire

1. Cut the piece of hide into an oval shape. You will want it to be big enough to wrap around your small, smooth rocks.

2. Cut or burn a small hole into each of the narrow ends of the oval. You can do this by heating a pencil-sized stick until it glows red and then burning through the hide, or you can cut or bore out the holes with an awl.

3. Peel the fibers of your plant apart and rub them between your fingers so that they thin and stretch. Braid them together, adding additional pieces of fiber for length as you braid, until you have formed a rope which can fit through the holes in the hide. Cut the rope into two

2-foot-long sections and tie one to each side of the hide by using the hole.

4. Stand with your non-dominant foot in front. Hold both ends of rope in your dominant hand and place a rock into the hide, pinching the hide around the rock to keep it in place. Raise both hands to eye level with the rope ends in your rear hand and the hide and rock in your front hand, pulling the rope taut. Your hands should be aligned and aiming at your target. Use your front hand as your sight. In one fluid movement, release the hand holding the hide and swing the sling once around your head, letting go of one of the rope ends as you come full circle on your swing.

HOW TO **MAKE AN ATLATL**

HE ATLATL is an under-the-radar tool that is believed to have originated in Europe, possibly Spain, that is used to throw a dart that's sort of a hybrid between an arrow and a spear. It's a force multiplier that allows more acceleration for a throwing weapon than a human can generate alone.

You will need:
- A fixed blade knife or hatchet
- A 4-to-5 foot long green stick about 1½ inches thick (for the dart)
- A 3-inch thick, 5-foot long tree limb or sapling with a branch growing out of it at a 45 degree angle (for the atlatl)
- Fire

1. Strip your green stick of any twigs, branches or bark. Carve one end to a point and square off the other into a flat end, beveling the edges. Whittle a small groove or shallow hole into the center of the squared-off end large enough to fit the end of the atlatl's spur. Harden the point in fire.

2. Cut the tree limb to the length of your own elbow to fingertips, making sure that the 45 degree branch is near one end. Peel off all the bark and strip it of any other twigs or branches. Using your knife or hatchet, carve it down to a flat surface (lengthwise) leaving the whole atlatl thick enough to be strong. The top will be the side with the 45 degree branch. Cut the branch down to about a 2-inch spur. Carve two 1-inch deep finger grooves into opposite shoulders of the atlatl on the far end from the 45 degree branch. Make sure to smooth all surfaces to avoid splinters.

3. Fit the flattened end of the dart to the spur of the atlatl and hold the atlatl in your dominant hand with the dart between your fingers. Stand with your non-dominant leg in front and the atlatl and spur between the second and third fingers of your hand, palm facing up. Raise them above your head and throw the dart off the atlatl as you would a spear.

HOW TO **MAKE A HAMMER**

UKE WAS undoubtedly handy with a hammer, and now you'll have the advantage of being able to make this versatile tool yourself. A hammer can split, chisel, pound, break, crush, flatten, drive and it can also be used to make other tools. Plus, if necessary, it can be used in self-defense.

You will need:
- A fixed blade knife
- A fist-sized rock or a heavy piece of wood
- A green sapling, about 18-inches long and 4-inches wide
- Fire

1. Have a seat and get comfortable. Lay your sapling down in front of you and set your knife into it like a nail, crosswise about a third of the way from one end. Take your rock or heavy piece of wood and pound the knife about an inch into the wood, take it out, rotate the sapling slightly, set the knife and repeat. Do it again and again until you've made a 1-inch cut all the way around the sapling.

2. Using your knife as a chisel, use the rock to pound the tip of your knife into the end of the sapling you wish to use as your mallet end. Chisel out pieces from the tip down to the 1-inch cut until you are down to a much smaller circumference. It should fit comfortably in your fist as a handle.

3. Peel the bark off the mallet end and use the rock to rub the entire hammer and handle smooth. You can also harden the mallet end with fire to reinforce it. You now have a field-expedient hammer or mallet.

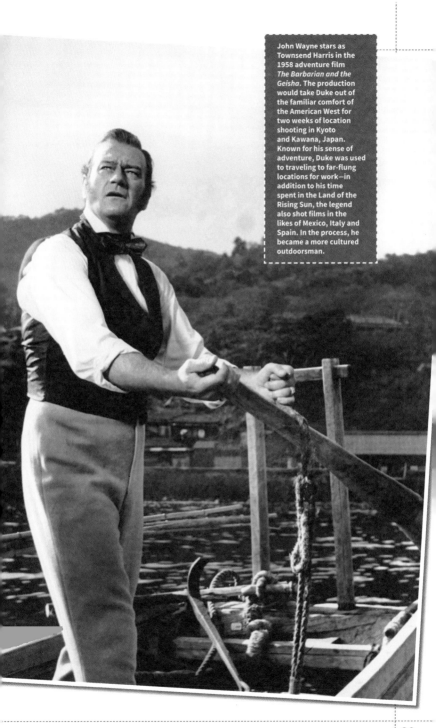

John Wayne stars as Townsend Harris in the 1958 adventure film *The Barbarian and the Geisha*. The production would take Duke out of the familiar comfort of the American West for two weeks of location shooting in Kyoto and Kawana, Japan. Known for his sense of adventure, Duke was used to traveling to far-flung locations for work—in addition to his time spent in the Land of the Rising Sun, the legend also shot films in the likes of Mexico, Italy and Spain. In the process, he became a more cultured outdoorsman.

HOW TO
MAKE AN AXE

 TRUE OUTDOORSMAN like John Wayne would never be caught out in the wilderness without an axe. Should you ever find yourself far away from civilization without this incredibly useful tool, this guide will help you craft your own axe so you can cut through the challenges you face with ease.

You will need:
- A fixed-blade knife
- A fist-sized rock or a piece of heavy wood
- A broad, flat river rock
- A large, unmoving rubbing rock
- Green sapling, about 3 to 4 inches thick
- Leather or sinew lashing
- Fire

NOTE While you can use flaked or chipped stone for your axe head, remember that it is breakable. It may be the sharpest option, but it's not the strongest.

1. Settle in, pilgrim—this is going to take a little while. Look at all sides of your rock and decide how to orient the axe head. Once you've determined the orientation, simply rub your river rock on the large stone and grind it down into the shape of an axe head. You will want the thick back side of the axe head to gradually narrow toward the blade end.

2. Strip the bark off your sapling and begin to create a divot into it about 6 to 8 inches from the top. Set the tip of your knife in the divot and use a rock or a piece of wood to hammer it part way in. Withdraw the knife before it gets stuck, set it next to your first divot and create a new divot with the knife and then hammer the knife into it again.

John Wayne and Jean Arthur in *A Lady Takes a Chance* (1943). The film is one of five in which the actor plays a character with his own moniker, Duke.

NOTE The goal is to create one large divot for the axe head via several smaller, adjacent divots. Keep repeating the process until you have a slot big enough to insert the back (thick end) of the axe head in snugly. Turn the whole thing blade-side up and set it on the ground. Use your hammering tool to hammer the handle down further around the axe head.

3. In most cases, the axe will be fit for use already. However, you can secure your axe head to the handle by tying your lashing material around it in an X pattern.

HOW TO **MAKE A WHISTLE**

SIGNALING FOR help comes in many forms, and the purpose is to generate something that can be detected by others using their sense of sight, hearing or smell. In a survival scenario such as the one seen in John Wayne's 1953 film *Island in the Sky*, the availability of a signal can save lives. Fortunately, you can make one of the most effective signals, a whistle, with materials easily found in the woods.

You will need:
 • An acorn top

1. Hold the acorn top, oriented like a bowl, in both hands.

2. Place both thumbs over the top of the bowl holding it between your thumbs and forefingers.

3. Leave a small gap for air between your thumbs, bring the lip of the bowl to your mouth and blow air through it with intent. A shrill whistle should sound. If not, alter your thumb position and try again. With practice you will be able to make a high-pitched sound that truly carries.

Alternatively, you can use a single blade of grass as a whistle if it is sufficiently wide. Place the piece of grass between both thumbs, stretching it taut and holding it between the fleshy base and the ends of your thumbs. There is a natural gap between the first and second joints of your thumbs and this is where you will blow. The grass acts like a reed in a woodwind instrument and emits a whistle if it is sufficiently taut.

John Wayne in the 1953 film *Island in the Sky*, which sees Duke as Capt. Dooley, the pilot of a C-47 transport plane called the Corsair. After icy winds cause the Corsair to rapidly lose altitude and radio contact, Capt. Dooley manages to land the falling plane in the unwelcoming frozen wilderness of Quebec. The film was initially scheduled to shoot in Big Bear in Southern California, but was relocated to Donner Lake, California, due to the original location's lack of snow. Authenticity was always a key ingredient when making a John Wayne film.

John Wayne and Lee
Aaker in *Hondo* (1953).

HOW TO MAKE A FISH HOOK

A **FISH HOOK** is an essential tool that can yield a delicious dinner, and it can also be made out of almost anything: a safety pin, soda can pull tab, paperclip, bobby pin, sewing needle, straight pin, thick wire, antenna, credit card sliver, large staple and many other things. Usually, you can find a usable material from the litter in your own pockets.

You will need:
- Any of the items listed on the opposite page
- Two small pieces of wood or sticks
- Fishing line, paracord, sinew or a plant with long fibers

1. Bend the material back and forth until you have broken it down to a length roughly equal to your thumb.

2. Use two pieces of wood or two sticks like pliers to hold onto the metal while you bend it into a hook.

3. Bend the non-pointed end into a little circle to give yourself a place to tie the line.

4. If you are using a soda can pop tab, simply cut into the rim at an angle and then cut out the insides. Then, cut a bit more of the rim away on the opposite side from your first angular cut to open up the hook area.

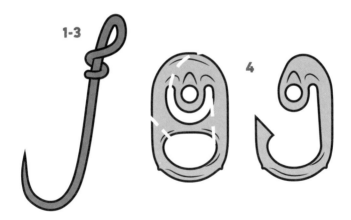

5. Feed your line through the little hole you made and tie it off. You can tie it to a stick or just use it as is.

NOTE If you cut the sheath off a section of paracord, you will find five to eight strands of individual line inside. This is an ideal line for fishing.

HOW TO
MAKE A TORCH

 INDING YOUR WAY in the dark can be one of the most difficult challenges you face in the great outdoors. Both simple and effective, a handmade torch can help guide you through the unlit landforms and foggy nights you might find yourself navigating through.

You will need:
- Oil, pine pitch or fat
- A piece of cloth
- A green stick about 2 feet long (preferably wet)
- Access to water
- Fire

1. Melt your pine pitch to liquid over a fire.

2. Soak the green stick in water to prevent what will become your torch handle from catching on fire.

3. Take your piece of cloth (you can use your own clothing) and wrap it around the top of the wet stick making sure to tie it securely. Try to keep all of the cloth confined to the top 4 to 6 inches of the wet stick.

4. Spread your pine pitch, oil or animal fat over the surface of the cloth and light it.

NOTE While carrying a torch, always ensure you have enough clearance not to catch anything above you on fire. Know which way the wind is blowing and watch for flying embers. Never take a lit torch into a cave unless the ceiling is significantly high above you, as heating the ceiling of an

John Wayne and Tyrone Power, Sr. in *The Big Trail* (1930).

otherwise cool cave can cause the rock to expand and even break off and fall.

CATTAIL TORCH

If you have access to a cattail reed, this will be a time saver. You can simply spread your animal fat, pine pitch or oil over the top half and light it. It blazes high and burns for a while.

HOW TO
MAKE A BOWL AND SPOON

 AKING A BOWL from scratch can be a bit of a patience tester, but the best things in life are worth waiting for. Once you start eating meals like a civilized citizen of the world again, you'll be glad you put the time and effort into this project.

You will need:
- A fire with embers
- A large, flat piece of wood at least 4 inches deep and 6 inches wide (for the bowl)
- A flat rock for scooping, about the size of your open hand
- A fixed-blade knife
- A foot-long section of wood about 2 to 3 inches deep and wide (for the spoon)

BOWL

1. Build your fire first—you will need hot embers to get started.

2. Strip the wood of all bark and flatten one side as much as you can.

3. Use your scooping rock to pull embers out of the fire and pile them up in the middle of your wood. Keep them contained to the center and leave an inch or more of border around the edges. Your bowl material might catch on fire—this is fine as long as you contain it to the area you are trying to hollow out. If it's a breezy day, this project will be done faster. If not, you can blow on the embers to keep them as hot as possible.

4. When the embers burn out, dump the ashes back into the fire and use your scooping rock to pull all the burnt material out of the bowl. By now you should have a concave surface. Pull new embers from the fire, place them in the shallow bowl and let them do their job. Repeat as many times as necessary to achieve the depth you need.

5. Clean the bowl out with your scooping rock and use it to rub the entire surface smooth so you don't eat any splinters.

SPOON

1. Making a spoon is very similar but on a much smaller scale. Starting with a 1-foot long section of wood, use your knife to strip the bark and carve 75 percent of the length down to handle-size. Put an ember or two on the thick part and start the process of burning out the spoon hollow. Use your rock to dig and smooth until you have a suitable cooking and eating utensil.

John Wayne and Beulah Bondi in *Back to Bataan* (1945).

HOW TO
MAKE A WATER FILTRATION SYSTEM

WITH THE RIGHT MATERIALS, even a greenhorn can build a portable water filtration system.

You will need:
- A plastic water bottle
- A clean sock
- A knife or multi-tool
- Charcoal (if available)
- Sand
- Small and large gravel
- Small rocks

To get started:

1. Cut the plastic bottom off the bottle and remove the cap. Turn the bottle upside down.

2. Cut the sock in half, then stuff the ankle half of the sock into the neck of the bottle.

3. Keeping the bottle upside down, add a layer of charcoal if available.

4. On top of the charcoal, add a layer of sand.

5. On top of the sand, add a layer of small gravel.

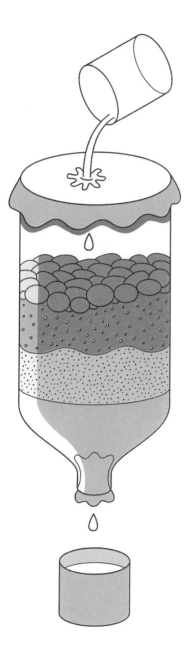

6. On top of the layer of small gravel, add a layer of large gravel or small rocks.

7. Stretch the toe half of the sock over the wide opening of the water bottle.

8. Pour water through the sock and into your filtration system.

Pour dirty water into the large opening and clean water will drip out of the small opening. The upper sock will screen out visible dirt and each layer of filtration will screen out smaller and smaller particles. It will take a little while to drip through.

At this point you have cleaned the water of dirt and debris but you must still boil it to kill the bacteria before drinking it.

HOW TO MAKE A LIFTING AND TIGHTENING SYSTEM

HETHER YOU'RE constructing a shelter, hanging a clothesline or trying to move a heavy load, being able to create an efficient lifting and tightening system can be an essential skill. Here's how to make a simple, all-in-one pulley, winch and hoist which you can use to move something heavy uphill.

You will need:
- Line (rope or paracord will work nicely) of about 3 times the length of the distance you wish to move something
- An immovable anchor point (a tree or rock outcropping)
- 2 carabiners

1. Take one end of your rope and tie it to your immovable anchor point using either a bowline (pg. 40) or a figure-eight knot (pg. 44). Attach one carabiner to the rope around the anchor.

2. Let your rope out as you walk it downhill toward the object, you wish to move. Tie the rope securely around the object taking care that it will not come dislodged with tension or loosened as you drag it. Attach the second carabiner to the line around your object.

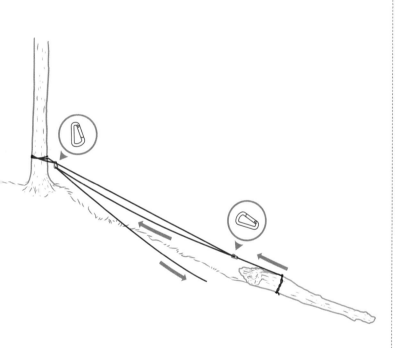

3. Run the loose end of your rope through the carabiner and back up to the anchor point up the hill. Run the rope end in your hand through the uphill carabiner and you now have a hoist. You can pull the rope hand over hand as you transfer the energy through the rope and into dragging the object to your position.

CONSTRUCTING CRIBBING AND RECOVERY DEVICES

 HAT HAPPENS when your vehicle is stuck beyond your ability to recover it with your own strength? Suppose there is someone trapped under a very heavy object that you cannot lift. Unless someone with the limitless strength of a John Wayne character comes along to help, you're going to need to use a system called cribbing. The point of cribbing is to use the largest material that will fit into the space below a heavy object to force it up.

You will need:
- Building materials such as logs, branches, sticks, planks, large rocks

1. Start by assessing how much space there is beneath the heavy object. Perhaps the object is a boulder and it is pinning someone to the ground. There is always space, even if it might only be measured in millimeters. Walk around the object and figure out where to begin cribbing. You will want to choose a place where your cribbing structure adds to the stability of the boulder and does not unbalance it.

2. Select the largest material you have that will fit into the space and work it underneath the load.

3. Take another piece of cribbing material and add it underneath the first one. This will push the object up. Take the third piece of cribbing material and push it in under the last one you added to push it up more. You are building a support structure from the ground up—each new piece you push in will take more and more of the load off. You may not see the boulder move by much, but the weight is slowly being transferred from the pinned victim to the cribbing.

4. As soon as you have just enough space, take a jacket, a rope or backpack straps and place them under the pinned person, around their back and under their arms. Use the straps to pull the person straight out from under the boulder without twisting or turning them at all.

NOTE You can use this cribbing technique to recover a stuck vehicle in certain situations as well. If one or more tires is in the air, you can build cribbing up to the tire to give it a surface upon which to gain traction.

HOW TO TIE A BOWLINE KNOT

HE BOWLINE knot is used as a no-fail anchor point. It can be used to tie one end of a rope to an anchor, such as a boulder or a tree, and it can also be used to tie a rope around yourself should you need to act as your own anchor.

You will need:
- The free-running end of a rope
- An anchor point (this can be your body)

1. Hold the free-running end in your non-dominant hand with your palm open and facing up. The tail should be pointing away from your body. With your dominant hand, grab the rope and twist it into an overhand bight by making one 180 degree twist away from your body. Leave enough tail for the knot. We will now refer to the free-running end of the rope as "the rabbit." The rabbit comes up through the hole you made.

2. The rabbit now goes up over the lip of the hole and "down the hill" toward the length of the rope. It then goes around the back of the length of rope and back up on the opposite side.

3. The rabbit goes back down through the hole. Pull it tight and you will have an anchor point around an object.

1

2

3

HOW TO **TIE** **A SQUARE KNOT**

 HE SQUARE knot is used for joining two like types of rope together, often to secure rappel seats and other similar applications.

You will need:
 • 2 free-running ends of the same type of rope

1. Leaving yourself enough tail of each end of rope, take one end in each hand with your thumbs facing up.

2. Memorize this simple rule: Left over right, then right over left. Take the rope in your left hand and and wrap it once around the other end making sure to go over the top.

3. Take the end now in your right hand and wrap it once around the other end, also by going over the top. If you can tighten the knot by pulling both ends and loosen it by pushing them together, you have a square knot. This complete knot resembles two interlocking horseshoes.

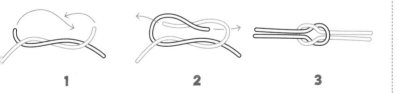

1   **2**   **3**

HOW TO TIE A ROUND TURN AND TWO HALF-HITCHES

HIS KNOT is used to rapidly attach the free-running end of rope to an anchor point. It can be used to rappel from an anchor or even to sling a hammock so you can kick back like Duke on a rare day off.

You will need:
- A free-running end of rope and an anchor point

1. Leaving at least 2 feet of tail, wrap the rope completely around your anchor point twice. This is your round turn.

2. Cross the extra 2 feet at the end over the front of the rope. Bring the tail up under and through the lower loop of your round turn. Tighten it.

3. Bring the tail across the top of the rope and back through the loop you just created. Tighten it again.

1

2

3

HOW TO TIE A HALF HITCH KNOT

 HALF HITCH is used to attach quickly to an anchor point, such as a hitching post or tree branch. It can also be used to add support to another knot: Simply take the loose end(s) of the existing knot and tie a half hitch to the main rope.

You will need:
* A rope

1. Take the free running end of your rope and loop it around the hitching post or tree branch.

2. Bring the free end up and over the main rope, then draw it through the loop you just created. Repeat a second time.

3. Your half hitch should look like the one shown in image number 3. Pull to tighten.

1

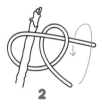
2

3

HOW TO **TIE A FIGURE-EIGHT KNOT**

HIS KNOT is used to tie into an anchor point. It works well for climbing and rappelling and when the person on belay must anchor themselves to the ground.

You will need:
- A rope

1. Take the free-running end of the rope and bend about 3 feet of it back on itself. Take the U-shaped end and cross it over the top of the rope. Flip the loop you just created over 180 degrees.

2. Take the U-shaped end of the rope and bring it up through the center of the hole.

3. Pull to tighten.

1

2

3

HOW TO TIE A GRAPEVINE KNOT

HIS KNOT is most commonly used to tie pieces of similar climbing rope together.

You will need:
- A rope

1. Bring the two free-running ends of the rope together so they overlap. Cross one of the ends over the other and wrap it around twice, creating two loops.

2. Take the resulting tail from the two loops and feed it through the top half of the first (nearest) loop and proceed through the top half of the second loop.

3. Using the resulting tail on the other side of the knot you just created, repeat steps 1 and 2. Pull on the rope to tighten the knots and slide them together.

1   2   3

HOW TO **TIE A TIMBER HITCH KNOT**

 AVING TROUBLE lifting that timber, pilgrim? This knot can help you move a log or other large piece of wood from one place to another.

You will need:
- A rope
- A log

1. Run the free end of the rope around the log, leaving yourself at least 3 feet to work with at the end. Cross the free end up and over the main line and pull it back through the loop.

2. Wind the free end of the rope around itself 4 to 5 times at the top of the log.

3. Pull all the slack out of the rope until it's tight.

1   2   3

John Wayne in *The Comancheros* (1961). Duke took over directorial duties for the film when director Michael Curtiz became too ill from his battle with cancer.

HOW TO **TIE**
A WATER KNOT

HIS KNOT is used to connect two ends of nylon tubular webbing to create a nonslip knot. It can be used for anchor points or Swiss seat harnesses.

You will need:
- Tubular nylon webbing

1. Take the free-running end of webbing and form an overhand knot.

2. Take the tail of the second piece of nylon webbing and follow the tail of the first knot into the hole. Trace the knot completely until you come out the other side. You are making just one knot with two ends of rope and it will look like you used the two simultaneously.

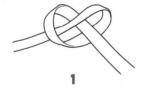

1

2

3

HOW TO TIE AN ALPINE BUTTERFLY KNOT

HIS KNOT is specifically used mid-line. It allows you to tie something or someone off when you have no access to either end.

You will need:
- The middle section of a rope

1. Take a loop of rope (a bight) in your hands—about 2 feet of mid-line rope is all you need. Hold the two sides of rope together in one hand and use the other hand to twist the U-shaped end 180 degrees. Pinch that together to make a loop in the rope. Go halfway up the loop and twist the loop another 180 degrees. It should look like a strand of DNA.

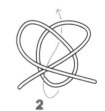

2. Keeping your original spot pinched, take the top of the second loop you made and bring it down and under the bottom of your pinch. Feed the end of the loop up through the hole you formed with the first loop.

3. Pull it tight.

HOW TO **TIE A TAUT LINE HITCH**

HIS HITCH is used to tighten line, and it's also very handy for constructing shelter when you need to set up a home away from home.

You will need:
- Paracord, rope or any kind of line
- An anchor point (like a tent stake)

1. Feed your line behind the anchor point leaving at least 1 foot of rope between the anchor point and the knot. You will need this space for tightening.

2. Cross the free end over top of the rope, reach through the top of the rope and grab the free end, bringing it through the loop. Do this twice.

3. Cross the free end of the rope across the two loops you made and over the top the length of rope. At this point, you should be working on the outside of your knot, on the opposite end from your anchor.

4. Run the end over top of the rope, around the back, and up through the hole you just made. You can slide the knot to add or take out whatever slack you need.

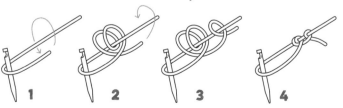

1   2   3   4

HOW TO TIE A CLOVE HITCH KNOT

 F YOU'VE ever seen John Wayne or any other cowboy tie their horse to a hitching post before heading into a saloon, this is the knot they used.

You will need:
- A rope
- A line to which you can hitch

1. Take the free-running end of your rope and place it over top the hitching line. Run it completely around, underneath to the left and over top to the right. It should form a Y.

2. Bring the free-running end over top of the hitching line and up through the center of the Y.

3. Pull it tight.

HOW TO **TIE A SQUARE LASHING KNOT**

HIS KNOT is used to join two hard materials together, such as two poles or a handle and an axe head. Whatever your needs may be, knowing how to tie this knot can make other important tasks much easier in the wilderness.

You will need:
- Lashing material (deer sinew, gut, fibrous plants)
- 2 poles to lash together

1. Lay one pole perpendicular to the other, one on top and one on the bottom. Tie a clove hitch around the vertical

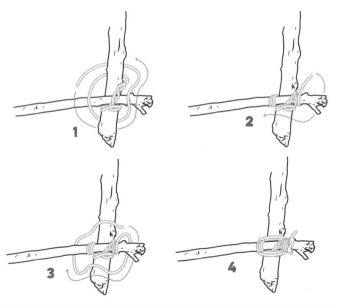

John Wayne in *The Long Voyage Home* (1940), which was based on a series of short plays by Eugene O'Neill.

pole with a free end of lashing. The knot should be on the same side as the horizontal pole.

2. After the clove hitch, run a free end of the lashing over the top of the horizontal pole, around the front of it and behind the vertical pole. This forms a repeating pattern that goes in front of the horizontal pole and behind the vertical pole. Repeat the whole circuit 2 to 4 times.

3. Using the remaining free end of lashing, begin on the side of the vertical pole opposite the clove hitch and wrap the lashing around the horizontal pole at the lashing material as tight as possible 2 to 4 times.

4. Finish the lashing with a second clove hitch on the opposite side from the first one.

HOW TO **TIE A SWISS SEAT RAPPEL HARNESS**

HIS IS a quick, easy and highly versatile option if you don't have a manufactured rappel harness. The rope you'll use can also be employed for something else after your rappel.

You will need:
  • 12 feet of climbing rope

1. Place the rope behind your back and bring the ends around in front of you so they're of roughly equal length. At your belly button, fold one end of rope over the other as if you're tying a shoe. Repeat this once more. Pull it tight. Let the two ends go.

2. Squat down, reach behind you and grab each end of rope. Bring the ends back between your legs.

1　　　　**2**　　　　**3**

John Wayne in *Circus World* (1964), which filmed on location in Barcelona, Spain.

3. Take each end of rope behind you and and wrap it around the rope waistband, making sure to go over the top of the rope. Feed the rope down from the top and pull away from your back to tighten.

4. Tighten the harness by squatting down and pulling down on the ends of rope. Stand up. Repeat the process of squatting, pulling and tightening a few times until it is almost uncomfortably tight.

5. Tie both ends of the rope into a square knot at your non-dominant hip. Tie one half hitch knot on each side of your square knot and tuck the tails into your pocket.

4   **5**

HOW TO **TIE A PRUSIK ASCENDING KNOT**

T TAKES true grit to climb a mountain, and it also takes a very secure rope. This knot can assist you in climbing.

You will need:
- 2 6-foot pieces of rope or paracord (for stirrups)
- 1 4-6 foot section of rope
- 1 12-foot section of rope (for Swiss seat rappel harness)
- An anchor point
- A hitching line
- 2 carabiners

1. Fold one piece of 6-foot rope in half and lay it over the top of your hitching line placing the two tails through the U-shaped end. Go around and through one more time so that there are a total of four layers on the hitching line. Tie a square knot and 2 half hitches into the two tails. Tighten it down. Repeat the entire process with your second 6-foot length of line next to the first one. You have just created stirrups.

2. Make and don a Swiss seat rappel harness (pg. 54).

3. Tie each end of your 4-6 foot rope into a figure-eight knot, creating a loop on each end. Clip one looped end into a carabiner and clip that carabiner to your harness. Clip the other looped end into the second carabiner and clip that carabiner into the upper (hand) stirrup. There should be enough slack for you to push the Prusik knots up the line while clipped in.

4. Put all of your weight onto your foot stirrup and slide the top stirrup up as high as you can. Shift your weight into your harness, bring the bottom stirrup up and repeat.

John Wayne and Sophia Loren in *Legend of the Lost* (1957). Exteriors for the film were shot in Libya while interiors were filmed at Cinecitta Studios in Rome.

FINDING FOOD & WATER

IF YOU KNOW WHERE
TO LOOK, THE GREAT
OUTDOORS CAN KEEP
YOUR BELLY FULL.

FORAGING

 OU WON'T be eating as well as Quirt Evans having breakfast in bed, but as long as you know what you're looking for, you can live off the land for a time. Foraging may only provide enough calories to keep the headaches at bay, and it requires a willingness to potentially eat something you consider gross in order to stay alive. Sorry, pilgrim, no pancakes.

You will need:
- Gloves to handle thorns and prevent stings
- A bag in which to collect your food

1. Make sure you know where you are—trespassing is illegal and foraging on someone's land is stealing. If you need what someone is growing, ask if you can take some.

2. Know what is likely to be growing during each season. For example, spring yields vegetables, nettles, flowers and weeds. Summer brings berries, roots, fruit and herbs. Autumn yields nuts, apples, peaches, certain berries and mushrooms. Winter brings sap, needles, pine cones, nuts, some mushrooms, some berries and wild garlic. While this is not a complete list, it should give you an idea of which seasons produce abundantly and which are lean.

3. Know where to look for what you need. It might be in the woods, along a fencerow, in a field, in a cave, on a tree or on the bank of a body of water. Educate yourself on what grows in your area. Some things can be eaten raw, some need to be cooked and some make great brews and stews. Read up on what grows where so you know where to look.

4. Above all, know what not to eat. Some things are merely inedible while others are poisonous to the point of being lethal. If you are in doubt about your safety, don't eat

John Wayne stars as Jacob McCandles in *Big Jake* (1971), which shot on location in Durango, Mexico, under the working title *The Million Dollar Kidnapping*. Duke's youngest son Ethan plays a major role in the film as "Little" Jake McCandles, the kidnapped grandson of the icon's titular character. Even as his children began taking part in the industry, John Wayne continued to put food on the table by working through his final years. As Ethan said in an interview, "The way he lived his life was exactly the work ethic you'd imagine for John Wayne."

it. If you are in a true survival situation and you have to give it a try, use the food edibility test (pg. 62).

EDIBLE OR NOT?

 F YOU'RE STRANDED far from civilization with no food, how will you determine what is or is not edible? It takes time and patience to learn which plants can be eaten in the wild, but as Breck Coleman reminds us in *The Big Trail*, "No great trail was ever built without hardship."

Here are the ground rules:

1. Do not eat anything for at least eight hours prior to the test, so that you can establish an accurate baseline.

2. Do not try more than one plant at a time.

3. Do not choose any type of fungus or anything with sap or milk.

4. Begin by selecting a plant that you believe will actually have some nutritional value.

5. Examine different parts of said plant. Some parts may be edible and others may be poisonous, so you'll have to test them separately.

6. Test the plant by rubbing each part of it on your skin, then watch for any kind of reaction. Wait 15 minutes before proceeding. If there's any kind of reaction, discontinue the test of that plant.

7. Rub a small piece of the plant gently on your lips and wait for five minutes, watching and feeling for a reaction.

8. Place a small piece of the plant in between your lower lip and your gum and hold it there for five minutes.

9. Chew the plant and hold it in your mouth without swallowing for 15 minutes.

10. Swallow the piece and wait for eight hours.

11. Eat half a cup of the plant and wait for an additional 8 hours.

12. If there are no reactions at any stage of the test, the plant is safe to eat.

Each person present can be assured that the plant is not poisonous after only one person conducts the test. However, this will not tell you if any person present is allergic to the plant. If a reaction happens at any point during the test, try to make yourself vomit, then drink plenty of water. Discontinue the test. Clear your system for eight hours, choose a different plant and start again. Make sure you choose a plant that's abundant in the area to be sure you'll have a consistent food source as you venture back to civilization. It may be a doozy of a test, but when it comes to staying alive, some things are worth the wait.

John Wayne and Stuart Whitman in *The Comancheros* (1961).

HOW TO **MAKE A SOLAR STILL**

 S ROBERT Hightower in *3 Godfathers* (1948) knows all too well, finding water in the desert can be a daunting feat. If you are in the desert without water rations, prioritize this project immediately after constructing your shelter. If you can, work on it after the sun goes down to help conserve your bodily fluids. You'll have to wait overnight for water to collect, anyway.

You will need:
- A large, clear, plastic tarp
- A vessel for collecting water
- The ability to dig

1. Dig a funnel-shaped pit. The opening should be just a little smaller than the surface of your tarp.

2. Place a collection cup, bowl, bag, etc., in the center of your pit.

3. Cover the hole of your pit with the tarp and seal the edges with dirt, sand, rock or any other weighted material you can scrounge. Place a weighted object like a rock in the middle of the tarp to create a funnel shape. Condensation will collect on the underside of the tarp and travel downward toward the point of the funnel. This is your collection point. Make sure the collection point is aligned with your cup or bowl so that the water drops right into it.

4. Go to sleep and check your basin for water in the morning. The deeper you dig, the more moist the sand or dirt will be and the more condensation it will produce.

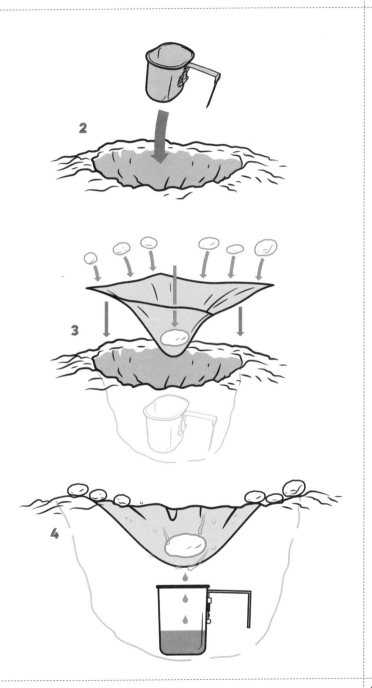

HOW TO **MAKE A BUSH STILL**

F YOU'RE in the wild with no water source available, you will need to use your understanding of condensation to create what you cannot find. The use of a bush still will not produce an abundance of water by any standards, but the goal here is to keep your body from dehydrating. Something small is better than nothing at all.

You will need:
- Several clear plastic bags (as large as possible)
- Access to bushes and/or trees

1. Choose low-lying bushes and trees as your targets. If you see cattail reeds, jewelweed, pond fronds or any other kind of water-reliant plant you are in a good spot. Willow trees, water maples and sycamores are all good choices. Make sure that chosen foliage has access to direct sunlight for at least part of the day.

2. Take as much of the bush or as many branches of the tree as you can bundle together and completely envelop them in your clear plastic bag. Tie the bag closed to seal the branches inside.

3. Wait, typically overnight. The water from the soil will be drawn up into the branches and condense on the leaves. With the plastic around it, the condensation will have nowhere to go and gravity will cause it to drip and collect in the bottom of the bag.

4. Make sure to keep the bottom area of the bag (the water collection point) clean and clear of any debris. This will be your drinking water. The more plastic bags you put out the more water you will collect. This is only a stop gap measure as you make your way toward an abundant source of water.

John Wayne stars as Ethan Edwards in *The Searchers* (1956). The John Ford Western is widely considered to be one of the best films of Duke's career, and its breathtaking setting plays a major role. Sprawling across 91,696 acres in Arizona and Utah, Monument Valley is best recognized by its vast landscapes and red rocks towering as high as 1,000 feet. Though the region has seen many droughts over the years, Ford didn't take chances—the director would hire a medicine man to bless the production with cooperative weather.

HOW TO **MAKE A WATER STILL**

SOMETIMES it takes water to make water. However, the original water does not have to be drinkable. With the aid of a water still, you can use pond water, sea water, even urine to pull clean water out of the air.

You will need:
- A soda can
- A plastic water bottle
- A knife

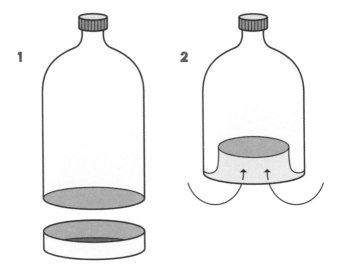

1. Fill the soda can half full with the non-drinkable liquid. Cut the bottom off the plastic bottle. Leave the lid on and securely closed.

2. Carefully curl the plastic around the bottom of the bottle inward, doubling it back on itself and creating a lip 1 to 2 inches deep.

3. Place the inwardly curled bottom of the bottle over the open soda can and press it down by a few inches. Place the whole thing in the sun and wait.

4. As the water in the soda can evaporates, it will condense on the inside of the bottle, run down the inside walls and collect in the tray you created. Take the bottle off the soda can, remove the cap and drink the condensation the same way you always drink from a plastic bottle.

TIPS FOR WATER TAPPING

 F YOU HAPPEN to have access to a river birch tree, Lady Luck is on your side. This tree makes tapping for water very easy, and it yields pure, safely drinkable water almost immediately. While there are other species of trees that will yield water such as sycamore, maple and bamboo, the river birch is the most efficient. You can find this tree in low-lying, wet areas and identify it by its papery bark and whitish color.

You will need:
- A fixed-blade knife (see pg. 8)
- A small stick (smaller than a pencil)
- A receptacle to collect the water
- A log, a rock or a branch to hold your receptacle high against the tree

1. Peel away a small section of bark, exposing a spot about the size of a quarter. Take your knife and set it at a sharp angle pointed upward, roughly 30 degrees out from the tree. Gently pound the tip of your knife into the tree about an inch. You can do this by striking the handle of the knife with your free hand.

2. When you begin to see water run down your knife and drip off the handle, you have gone far enough. Shave the ends of your small stick flat to channel the water where you want it to go. Remove your knife and replace it with one end of your small stick. The water should now run down the stick and drip off the end.

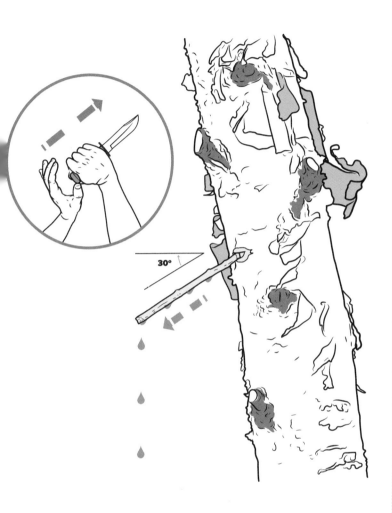

30°

3. Place your receptacle under the drip and place your log, branch or rock underneath to prop it up and keep it in place.

4. Wait. One drip at a time means this will take a while. For best results, wait overnight and check your receptacle in the morning.

TECHNIQUES FOR CARRYING WATER

 N SOME CASES, securing a source for hydration is only part of the process. You may have to travel to find water, at which point carrying it becomes the next part of the challenge.

Bamboo has sealed joints with water in each section, so if you're fortunate enough to find bamboo, you'll have both your water source and a way to carry it all in one. Treat each section of bamboo like a ready-made cup. If you simply want a sip, you can tap a hole in one section right above a joint and drink the water. If you want to make a cup, you can cut the bamboo in two places, right below one joint and right below the next closest joint. But if you don't have access to bamboo, you can use some unconventional methods for hauling H_2O:

You will need only one of the following:
- A non-lubricated condom
- A gourd, pumpkin or squash of some sort
- Windbreaker jackets
- Dried animal skin, bladder or intestine
- A plastic bag (as large as possible)
- Clay

1. Water is heavy and each type of container will only carry so much before it gives out. Experiment to see what yours can handle.

2. If you choose to use a non-lubricated condom or an

animal part, it will stretch considerably to accommodate a surprising amount. Simply fill the balloon-like material and tie off the end for ease of carry.

3. If you have a plastic bag or a windbreaker, you can line the inside of some tree bark or a hollowed out log with it for waterproofing. Remember that if the water line exceeds the plastic bag or windbreaker's coverage area it will leak or spill.

4. If there's clay in the ground, you can fashion a cup or container in short order. Wet clay will make the water dirty, so if you have time, form your clay cup and let it dry in the sun or near a fire before you use it. If you don't have time, try not to agitate the water as you carry it to minimize the amount of clay particles mixing into it.

5. If you find a gourd, pumpkin or squash, luck is on your side. Cut the narrow end off and hollow out the inside, getting rid of as much of the pulp and seeds as you can. Fill it with water and carry it with you.

John Wayne and Peter Ortiz (center) *in Rio Grande* (1950).

LINE AND HOOK FISHING TECHNIQUES

HILE YOU MAY not be quite as masterful as John Wayne on the *Wild Goose*, you can still successfully fish with just line and a hook.

You will need:
- Fishing line (string, monofilament, paracord or even fibrous plants will work)
- A hook (see pg. 28)
- A tree branch or stick (for the rod, optional)

1. If you can get to an elevated vantage point like a high bank, a rock or a bridge, you'll be able to see through the water more clearly.

2. You can use whatever kind of bait presents itself in that area: grubs, worms, insects or even smaller fish. Tie your line tightly to your hook and put the bait on the hook.

3. Place or cast your baited hook onto the water and wait. If you have a high vantage point and a good view of the water, choose a spot where the fish congregate. If not, you may have to try several different spots or various times of day to get a catch.

4. If you wish to turn your attention elsewhere while you wait and you don't have a rod, you can tie the end of the

John Wayne as Army dispatch rider Hondo Lane and Lee Aaker as Johnny Lowe in *Hondo* (1953). While Johnny does know how to fish, he admits he doesn't know how to swim. Upon hearing that, Hondo decides to teach the boy the old-fashioned way by tossing him into the water and shouting instructions. Fittingly, Duke had a knack for guiding the young actors he worked with to success. Aaker would go on to star as Cpl. Rusty on *The Adventures of Rin Tin Tin* and appear on several other series such as *The Lone Ranger* in 1955 and *The Lucy Show* in 1963.

line to your big toe. You will feel it when you get a tug.

5. A rod is not necessary, but it can give you extra reach, the option to put the line down while you wait and additional techniques to draw in your catch.

HOW TO **CATCH A FISH WITH YOUR HANDS**

NOTHING SIGNIFIES the challenge of surviving in the wild more than the endless struggle between man and fish—a contest pitting ingenuity and patience against speed, strength and instinct. But while spearing a big one or reeling it in with a hook and line you made yourself is certainly impressive (and in most cases, ideal), sometimes you're left with no other option but to snatch some dinner with your bare hands.

1. Once you've spotted your prey, you should have an idea of what you might be up against. Some fish are slower and easier to catch, while others will fight you to the finish. Catfish are particularly nasty opponents, armed with natural defenses capable of slicing up your hands should your attack be poorly placed. Trying to wrest such a fish from the water is a challenge at best, and a humbling experience for many, as catching one with slick, bloody hands is nearly impossible.

2. While it may seem logical to get all the way in the water, this can be a disadvantage as it makes it easier for the fish to sense your presence. Instead, search for a bank overlooking a slow-moving tide. Position yourself so that you're certain not to fall in, then lean down and submerge your arm until the water is just above your elbow. Be still and wait. Fish won't go near any object that's warmer than the water it's swimming in, so you'll need to wait for about

John Wayne and his son Michael show off some freshly caught lobsters in Hawaii.

15 minutes, at which point your arm will stop emitting heat and the fish will find it difficult to tell the difference between you and the underwater vegetation.

3. Wiggle your index finger as if it were a worm on a hook in order to lure the fish. The fish will assume it's seeing a smaller fish, an insect or some other food source and be lured into your grasp.

4. Once the fish is closing in, aim your fingers under its gills and grab it quickly and firmly. You'll find a lot of bone and cartilage in that spot, which will make it easier to hold onto the fish and keep it from wriggling away.

HOW TO **CLEAN, SCALE AND GUT A FISH**

 NCE YOU'VE CAUGHT your fish, keep it cold and wet until you're ready to clean it. Make sure you don't wait longer than an hour or two. Though prepping a fish is a messy process, it's well worth the wait. Just be sure to dispose of the remains properly (pg. 100) to avoid unwanted visitors at your campsite.

You will need one of the following:
- A knife (pg. 8)
- A bucket or receptacle (for the fish parts)
- Gloves (optional)

1. SCALE THE FISH Holding the fish firmly by the tail on a flat surface, use your knife to scrape the scales off, working from the tail toward the gills. Be careful not to exert too much pressure as doing so can gash the fish.

2. RINSE THE FISH Once you've cleared the scales from both sides of the fish, rinse it with clean water (pg. 70). When applying the water, be careful not to use too much pressure. Fish meat is fragile and can be damaged by rough handling, so take 'er easy.

3. MAKE THE MAIN CUT Carefully insert the knife at the base of the fish near the tail, and draw it toward the head. This will split the fish up the middle. If you're working with a small fish, hold it down on its side with

In his rare free time, John Wayne loved to take his family and friends out on the open sea via his beloved yacht, a decommissioned Navy minesweeper called the *Wild Goose*. But as Ethan Wayne recalls, the children still had chore duties while on the boat. When Duke and his pals went fishing during an outing, they were known to reel in quite a collection of aquatic life—and the unpleasant part of the seafood prep process was Ethan's responsibility. "If they caught a bunch of fish, I'd be gutting fish for an hour," the legend's youngest son remembers.

one hand while cutting it. If your catch is larger, place it on its back for the cut

4. **REMOVE THE GUTS** With one hand, use your fingers to open up the cut you've just made. Reach in with your other hand and pull out the entrails, placing them in your bucket or other container reserved for the fish guts.

5. **RINSE THE CAVITY** Rinse the inside of the fish with clean water, and then rinse the outside for a second time.

6. **REMOVE THE HEAD** *(Optional)* Some fish are cooked with the heads on. Many pan-sized fish are not. If you choose to remove the head of your fish, cut it off behind the gills.

SPEAR FISHING TECHNIQUES

 FISHING SPEAR can be as simple as a sharpened stick or as complicated as a four-pronged spear (pg. 10). The technique for throwing the spear is largely the same for both, but the technique for drawing your catch out of the water is different.

1. While you can fish blind with a line and hook, you need to be able to see the fish when spearing. You can accomplish this by finding a high vantage point or standing up to your knees in shallow water.

2. Water distorts images through refraction and reflection, so you'll need to aim the tip of your spear just below where the fish appears to be. Aim to spear through the broadest part of the fish.

3. Fish are quick, so you'll need to be quicker (and undetected). If you're standing in the water, do not disturb it before thrusting your spear. If you are clearly visible from your vantage point, do not make any radical movements before thrusting your spear. Stand ready to throw so the fish has very little time to react.

4. If you're working with a simple sharpened stick rather than a barbed or four-pronged spear, the fish can slip off once it is skewered. To avoid this, dip your arm low into the water and raise the spear end up with care to keep hold of your fish.

THE BEST FISH FOR SPEARING

HILE SPEAR FISHING takes time and practice and isn't exactly easy from the get-go, certain fish are more susceptible to spearing than others. If you're able, research the area before heading out to see what species are abundant so you get an idea of what to look for when you're peering into the water.

PIKE

Pike are plentiful, and you can identify them by their long, somewhat narrow bodies that are greenish-brown in color. They tend to search for food in weedy, shallow waters, which is perfect for when you're spearfishing from a vantage point.

CARP

This fish is common in North American lakes, and they can be quite large, which means a bigger target and more food for you. Carp are also known to be slow swimmers, which works in your favor.

CATFISH

Identified by the long, whisker-like feelers around their mouths, catfish are common throughout rivers and lakes in North America. While they can be quick, their speed only lasts for short bursts, so try to catch one as it becomes fatigued.

BOW HUNTING TECHNIQUES

HERE'S NO SHORTCUT to becoming a proficient bow hunter, especially if you've just made your very first primitive bow. Practice, practice, practice, pilgrim. In the meantime, use these tips to make your practice and performance more efficient.

1. When making your own arrows (pg. 14), you'll want the heads to be as fine and sharp as possible. It's better to have a needle point on a small projectile than to have something bigger but duller.

   The perfect ratio would be a 30-inch arrow and a .11-ounce arrowhead. Try to get as close to this as you can.

2. Speed equals penetration. The faster you can make the arrow fly, the more work it will do for you. Longer draws transfer more energy, so make sure your bow allows for a significantly long draw. A primitive bow will only have around a 50-pound draw, which already puts you at a disadvantage.

3. There is a saying in Special Forces: "Aim small, miss small." The better your targeting the more success you will have. As you practice, try to get your shot placement consistently into a 1-to 2-inch grouping. If you can consistently do that, even your misses will be close to your target.

RECOVERING ARROWS

SSUMING RESOURCES will be scarce when you begin your bow hunting experience, you won't want to waste arrows. Even if you miss wildly and end up shooting a tree rather than a moving target, you can still recover an arrow without damaging it.

1. If you're new to bow hunting, most of your misses will result in arrows on the ground in the vicinity where you were aiming. And since your arrows are made of natural materials like those found on the ground, watch your step so you don't end up finding an arrow by snapping it.

2. If your arrow gets stuck in a tree trunk or stump, you can sometimes recover it by peeling away the area around the arrowhead. Never use your knife for this, as you might break the blade. If you have pliers, you can use them to pull the surrounding bits of bark out until the arrowhead is loose enough to pull out. Otherwise, you can dig it by carefully removing the bits of bark by hand.

3. Occasionally you'll get lucky and the arrow won't be too deep in the tree trunk. If only the tip is stuck and you can still see the base of the arrowhead, you may be able to gently turn the arrow counterclockwise to remove it, just as you would to unscrew something.

HOW TO **BUILD A FISH TRAP**

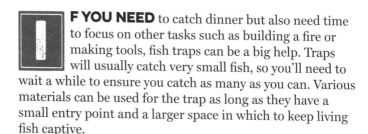

F YOU NEED to catch dinner but also need time to focus on other tasks such as building a fire or making tools, fish traps can be a big help. Traps will usually catch very small fish, so you'll need to wait a while to ensure you catch as many as you can. Various materials can be used for the trap as long as they have a small entry point and a larger space in which to keep living fish captive.

You will need one of the following:
- A woven basket
- A water bottle
- A net
- Rocks, sand, mud or clay

1. If you're using a basket, a bottle or a net, place it horizontally in shallow water where small fish collect and weight it down with rocks so it does not float away. The opening should be positioned so the water flows into it. Fish may enter the trap because they're curious, they're seeking covered shelter or because they came in on a current and can't swim against it to escape.

2. If you're using rocks, sand, mud or clay, your trap will be more like building a tiny retaining wall. Lay your foundation under water and build it up—either against a pre-existing surface, such as a large, flat-sided rock or the bank of a river, or as a nearly-closed structure unto itself—until the top of the wall is above the water line. Make sure the only opening is the fish entry point.

3. When it comes time to collect the fish from inside the

John Wayne and Sam in the 1953 John Farrow film *Hondo*.

retaining wall, the space inside the trap should be small enough that you can use your hands or a piece of cloth or net to scoop the fish out. If you have submerged a material trap, you can collect the fish by drawing the entire contraption out of the water. If you plan to be in one spot for a while, empty the trap and replace it so it begins to collect fish again.

SPEAR HUNTING TECHNIQUES

 HERE ARE TWO primary considerations when spear hunting: You must choose between stalking and still hunting. Stalking requires silent movement and the ability to stay upwind of your prey, but it affords more opportunities to spot prey. In either case, spears have a finite range and must not be confused with the capabilities of bow or firearm hunting.

1. If you are going to stalk, go slow. Keep your weight on your back foot and use your front foot to probe ahead of you for anything that might make a noise. When you shift your weight forward, place it on your heel first and then roll onto your toes to avoid making noise. Watch for anything growing or hanging from the ground up to your head that might produce noise if you brush against it. Stick close to trees, bushes, rocks or a ridge line that can help obscure your silhouette. As you move along, keep a lookout for animal droppings, tracks and broken branches for an indication of what is around and which direction it went.

2. Still hunting requires you to be able to remain still for long periods of time, to know from which direction your prey will approach and to choose a spot upwind. It may require some camouflage of sight or even scent. Generally, it's best to find a high vantage point which allows you to see for greater distances than you would if you waited on the ground.

3. There are two primary methods of spearing an animal. One is to throw the spear as a projectile and make the kill

John Wayne stars as Ethan Edwards in the 1956 John Ford Western *The Searchers*. For much of the film, the quest to find his captured nieces Lucy (Pippa Scott) and Debbie (Natalie Wood) is less of a search and more of a hunt. Still exhibiting lingering rage from the Civil War, the weathered Confederate operates with a sense of fury and frets that Debbie may have embraced the lifestyle of her Comanche captors. Fortunately, he comes to his senses and is able to bring the girl home safely. It's an important reminder that a less aggressive approach can be key to a successful hunt.

from a short distance away. The other is to fall upon your prey from a height and drive the spear in by hand. Always do your best to kill the animal with a single thrust.

KNIFE HUNTING TECHNIQUES

 S WITH SPEAR hunting, knife hunting requires you to take all the precautions of stalking or still hunting. Remember that a knife is not a reaching weapon, and without skill and plenty of practice, it is not a projectile weapon either. That means you need to be close enough to touch your prey in order to kill it by stabbing it or slitting its throat.

1. Make sure your knife is thick, heavy and strong and has a fixed blade. In a perfect world, it would have grooves, holes or channels to break suction and allow for blood flow.

2. Always have a backup knife in case one is lost, broken or out of commission.

3. Keep your knife as sharp as possible. Keep it clean and carry it in a protected way. You can use oil to clean, protect and lubricate your knife.

4. Do not attempt knife hunting unless you are in very good physical shape and confident in your own ability to handle and treat any wounds you might sustain. An animal close enough for you to touch can wound you with its teeth, tusks, horns, antlers, hooves or anything else it has. Respect its strength, speed and capabilities.

Tully Marshall as Zeke and John Wayne as Breck Coleman in Raoul Walsh's epic 1930 Western *The Big Trail*. The film marked the first time Duke was cast as a leading man, and it remains one of the greatest cinematic depictions of the legend as a fearless outdoorsman. While his main mission is to find his friend's murderer, fur trapper Breck Coleman also puts his hunting skills to use on several occasions as he and a group of pioneers travel West. In one memorable scene, Breck and his scouts take down a herd of Buffalo to provide meat for the wagon train.

HOW TO
BUILD SNARES AND TRAPS

 HERE ARE MANY types of snares and traps, and each can be used for hunting, self-defense or a combination of both. Some merely trap while others trap and kill. Some require movable parts and others only require space and time. Remember where your snares and traps are set and how they work lest you succumb to your own inventions. Know what you intend to catch, how big it is, how it moves and where it might go.

You will need:
- About 20 sharpened sticks
- A shovel or a way to dig
- A heavy rock or log
- Cordage
- Twigs
- Bait

1. If you have a way to dig a pit and camouflage the opening, you can make a very simple trap. Collect around 20 sticks and sharpen them all to a point. Stick them into the ground in the bottom of the pit, pointy side up. You can add them to the walls of the pit as well to prevent uninjured prey from escaping by climbing. A punji pit can trap a wide range of animals and is only limited by the size of the pit.

2. You can make a deadfall trap by selecting a heavy rock or log and propping one end up precariously with twigs that will snap when the animal touches them. Just put bait under the elevated rock log and wait. This will only work for very small game such as rats, mice and small rabbits. You can also make a live-catch version by using a hollow container to catch instead of a rock or log to smash.

3. You can capture prey live by hollowing out a rotten log and positioning it at a slight angle on a stick that acts as a fulcrum. Place a good sized stick underneath the hollow log, perpendicular to the log and in the center. The log should be resting on the stick, one end higher than the other like a seesaw at rest. The lowered end should have an opening and the higher end should be closed off. Place bait inside the log. Once an animal enters the trap and triggers the seesaw action, you can close off the open end with net, screen, clothing, wood or any other material as long as it covers the open end of the log.

4. Never intentionally make an animal suffer. If you must kill, do so as quickly and humanely as possible.

TIPS AND TRICKS FOR TRACKING

 ITH ANY KIND of hunting, trapping or tracking it is imperative that you have a general sense of what kind of wildlife lives in a given area. You can expect to find wolves and bears in the tundra, deer in the timberland, bison on the prairie, cougars in the mountains and alligators in swamps. Once you narrow down your quarry, you can look for signs of its presence.

1. Tracks will tell you what is around, how many are traveling together, when they were there and which way they were going. Droppings also help you identify species.

2. Lighting plays a major role in tracking. You need to know how much of it you can expect and from what angles it will originate at different times.

3. Do not step on the tracks, droppings, broken foliage or any other sign the animal has left behind in case you lose the trail and need to go back and reconstruct it.

4. Green Berets are taught to use all of their senses. Sight, sound and smell are particularly useful for tracking, and you never know which sense may pick up on the clue and help you anticipate your quarry's movements.

5. Know that these techniques take time to perfect. Spend time practicing outdoors. Do some research on your area to figure out what lives there and what tracks it leaves.

John Wayne's Ethan Edwards examines the area in the 1956 classic *The Searchers*. As a Civil War veteran, Edwards alone is equipped to track down enemies and lead search-and-rescue missions. But as this mission is especially personal as it involves his own family, the Confederate is fortunate to have a skilled set of searchers by his side. The crew includes Texas Rangers Captain Sam Clayton (Ward Bond) and Mose Harper (Hank Worden), a weathered Indian scout, both of whom bring a wealth of much-needed experience to the search.

TIPS AND TRICKS FOR TRACKING *continued*

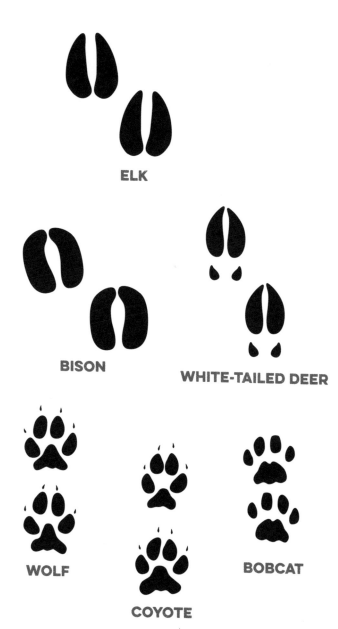

ELK

BISON

WHITE-TAILED DEER

WOLF

COYOTE

BOBCAT

RACCOON

COUGAR

GRIZZLY

SKUNK

HOW TO **FIELD DRESS GAME**

 NCE YOU'VE successfully hunted game, you still have a few chores to take care of before the animal can become your next meal. As a general rule, you'll want to gut the animal soon after killing it to avoid spoilage—especially in warm weather. To keep the meat clean, you can wait to skin the animal until you're ready to begin the cooking process.

You will need:
- A knife (pg. 8)
- A bucket or receptacle (for the organs)
- Gloves (optional)

GUTTING BIG GAME (DEER, ELK)

1. Lay the animal on its back with the spine straightened and the legs pointed upward. On one side of the anus, puncture the skin about 1 inch. Keeping the knife level, cut a whole around the anus (if the animal is female, include the vaginal opening in this cut). Then use the tip of your knife to cut the connective tissue holding the colon in place.

2. Begin at the top of the anal incision and cut upward through the hide until you've reached just above the pelvis. Do not cut through the abdominal wall. Slice down through the muscle until your knife touches the pelvic bone.

3. Starting at the top of the brisket (the chest area below the neck), make an incision down the underside until you reach the opening exposing the pelvic bone. Take care not to cut too deep in order to avoid puncturing organs.

4. At the bottom of the rib cage, make a cut through the abdominal muscles just shallow enough to fit your index and middle fingers. Lift the abdominal muscles with your fingers facing up to keep them away from the stomach, then slice through the lining following the line you made on the hide. Stop when you've reached the pelvic area at the bottom of the abdomen.

5. Pull the cavity open and find the diaphragm—the taut membrane separating the lungs and heart from the liver, stomach and intestines. Cut the diaphragm away from the interior walls of the body cavity, revealing the spine below.

6. Use your free hand to carefully reach up into the neck and grab onto the esophagus, which should feel like a ribbed vacuum hose. With your knife hand, cut through the esophagus just above where your other hand is holding it. Set your knife down and wrap both hands around the esophagus and pull firmly through the abdominal cavity until all the innards have come out. NOTE: If the bladder appears full, gently guide it out and away from the carcass to avoid it leaking onto the meat.

7. Flip the carcass onto the belly and splay the legs to drain the blood.

GUTTING SMALL GAME (SQUIRRELS, RABBITS)

1. Lay the animal on its back. Being careful to avoid slicing into the organs, make a shallow incision from the top of the sternum to the anus.

2. Cut the flesh vertically at the pelvis and splay the rear legs. Sever and remove the exposed rectum.

HOW TO FIELD DRESS GAME *continued*

3. Carefully open the upper chest cavity enough to reach and remove the internal organs.

4. Slice off and discard any bloodshot areas of flesh.

SKINNING BIG GAME (DEER, ELK)

NOTE This process is most efficient if you're able to hang the carcass by its rear legs, but it can also be accomplished with the animal on the ground.

1. Begin by finding the joints at the bends of each leg and cutting horizontally around the circumference of the leg, right on the center of each joint. From those cuts, make longer cuts that extend up the insides of the legs and reach the gutting incision on the belly.

2. Work the hide up from the flesh around the rear legs, separating it from the attaching muscle as needed with your knife blade.

3. When you have enough hide to get a good grip, roll the fur side underneath itself and pull down to the front shoulders. Use your knife to separate the remainder of the hide from the various joints and continue pulling away until you reach the throat.

4. If you have a sharp and strong enough tool, cut off the head. Otherwise, continue cutting the hide around the neck until you can completely remove it from the carcass in one piece.

SKINNING SMALL GAME (SQUIRRELS, RABBITS)

1. With your knife, slowly slice just above the waist and make a complete circle around the body. Be careful not to cut into the muscle beneath the hide.

2. Pull the top and bottom halves of the hide off of the

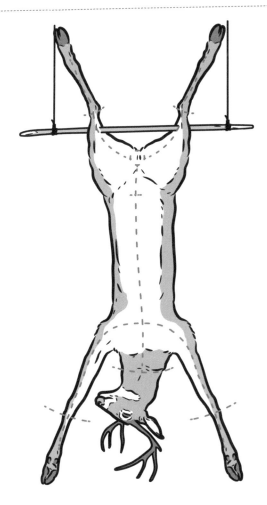

animal as if removing a shirt and pants. The connecting tissue is quite strong, so pull hard. Stop pulling when the bottom hide meets the ankles/base of the tail and the top hide meets the neck.

3. Sever the ankles, tail and head at the joints, then cut each limb off of the torso and cut the ribs from the spine.

4. To clean the meat, rinse with water or snow.

HOW TO **DISPOSE OF FOOD**

 VERY HIKER, CAMPER AND HUNTER knows you can't allow the enticing scent of food to linger in your vicinity overnight without expecting a visit from foragers and predators. Sure, the foragers are merely a nuisance, but the predators can be downright dangerous.

Here are some tips for disposing of carcasses or other food-related items to help you keep a low profile in the wild.

LAND DISPOSAL

1. Dig a cylindrical hole 2 feet deeper than the length of the carcass you need to bury. If you have already removed any organs, drop those into the hole first.

2. Then—and don't be squeamish—lower the body into the hole headfirst to push the organs which produce the strongest scent deepest underground.

3. Exit the hole, then fill it in with all the dirt you dug up and pack it down as tightly as you can.

THERMAL DISPOSAL

If you're planning ahead, perhaps for a long-term stay off the grid, the thermal disposal method is a great option. You will need:

- A 50-gallon metal drum
- Jet A fuel (you can buy Jet A at most municipal airports)

1. Check the weather for wind direction and speed. Select a site that is safe for fire building and does not risk starting a wildfire.

2. Place the carcass in the barrel and fill the barrel halfway with jet fuel.

3. Stand back, light the fuel and be prepared to tend the site for two hours.

In about two hours, even the bones and teeth will have turned to powder. This method produces a lot of smoke and smell, so be sure to protect yourself against smoke inhalation.

CAUTION The heat produced with this method will be extreme. Only use it if you've been trained how by a knowledgeable professional or an experienced hunter first.

WATER DISPOSAL
You will need:

- Something to act as weight
- Cloth, a tarp or plastic
- Chicken wire

1. Take the carcass and wrap it in perforated cloth, perforated tarp or perforated plastic along with the material you selected for weight. This can be rocks, metal, bricks, cement, cinder blocks or any other heavy object.

2. Spread the objects lengthwise along the carcass to ensure it will evenly stay underwater. The perforations will allow trapped air to escape.

3. After the carcass and weights are wrapped in the perforated material, wrap the outside in chicken wire to prevent parts of the carcass breaking off and returning to the surface.

4. Take your package away from shore and drop it into the water as gently and evenly as possible.

John Wayne in *A Lady Takes a Chance* (1943). The film's working titles were *Rodeo Story*, *The Cowboy and the Lady* and *Free for All*.

MAKING & MAINTAINING FIRE

LEARN THESE BASICS SO YOUR CAMPFIRE DREAMS DON'T GO UP IN SMOKE.

THE PRINCIPLES OF FIRE

 NCE YOU UNDERSTAND the key principles of fire, you can solve any problems created by the setting, elements, weather or materials you're working with. Fire requires three things: oxygen, fuel and an ignition source. Oxygen is found in the air around you and in the air you exhale with every breath. Air is 21 percent oxygen and 78 percent nitrogen plus a few traces of mixed gases which make up the remaining percent. Human beings inhale 21 percent oxygen from the air and metabolize about 4 percent, exhaling 17 percent back into the atmosphere. You can use that 17 percent to your advantage to help your fire catch and grow.

Fuel is technically anything that burns. There are short duration fuel sources such as tinder and kindling, and longer duration fuel sources such as logs. In order to properly build a sustainable fire, it's important to have a solid understanding of how to structure your fire materials. Tinder is a small amount of very dry and easily ignited materials, such as dry pine needles, birds nests, dry heather, dry leaves and dry grasses. This is what you will light with your ignition source. Tinder bridges the gap between the original spark and the kindling. Kindling is fuel of a greater size and duration than tinder that bridges the gap between tinder and logs, and can be materials such as twigs, pine cones and small branches. The spark created by the ignition source might come from flint, matches, a lighter, friction or another similar source. When the spark meets oxygen, the tinder catches on fire. The tinder catches the kindling and the kindling catches the large fuel source (which would be the log in this example).

As you build a fire, it's very important to remember fire
needs oxygen. Allow gaps and channels for air to flow
through in order to keep your fire fed. The more air that
blows through, the larger the fire will be. This is especially
important to remember on a windy day as wind can cause
a fire to blaze dangerously high or out of control. Always be
prepared to control your fire and never leave it unattended.
You can mitigate what the wind may do by choosing a
sheltered site for your fire pit.

If you're having trouble igniting your tinder or your fire
is threatening to die out, you can breathe life back into it
by gently blowing across the base. If you're trying to get
a spark to catch, be aware of the balancing act between
supplying crucial oxygen and not allowing the force of the air
to extinguish the attempt. The best way to understand fire
mechanics is to practice building fires in various conditions
to see what works and what doesn't.

TYPES OF TINDER

INDER IS widely available in some places but scarce in others. It's small and light and easy to carry, so it's best to keep some on you when you venture out into the wilderness. You can buy manufactured tinder or you can make tinder packs with castoff materials.

Before heading out on the trail, take an **empty toilet paper roll** (A) and stuff it full of dryer lint. Seal it in a plastic bag and put it in your pocket. This makes great tinder. However, if you have pets and there is hair and fur mixed into the lint, it will be much more difficult to light. In this case, you may want to opt for an alternative method. Gather some cotton balls and soak them in melted petroleum jelly, then place them in a sealed container so they don't make anything else greasy. They will catch a spark easily and burn nicely as tinder.

Char cloth (B) is another good tinder option, and one you can make in the field if you have the right materials. You will need a piece of cotton or linen fabric and a sealable metal box. Place the material in the box and place the box in the hot coals of a fire. The material will dry out and turn black but not ignite. In that state, it makes excellent tinder for a future fire.

You can also collect tinder by simply gathering small, dry materials and putting them in your pocket as you move along throughout the day. This is referred to as a **bird's nest** (C). As you pick up the likes of dry grasses and pine needles, ball them up together and hollow out the middle until you have a bowl-shaped nest. When it comes time to use it, you can place your spark right in the middle of the bowl.

You can make a **feather stick** (D) by shaving a dry stick until the pieces curl downward but allow them to remain attached to the stick itself. This gives you more surface area to catch on fire and the thin shavings ignite more easily than the solid stick.

No matter which method or materials you use, it may take a surprising amount of tinder to ignite your kindling, so always gather more than you think you'll need. And of course, if you have any unused portions once the flames are going strong, save those for future fires.

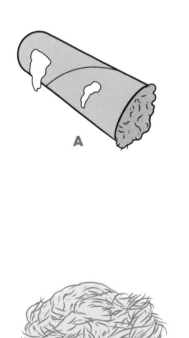

A

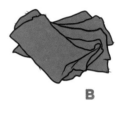

B

C

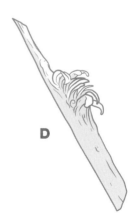

D

TYPES OF IGNITION

THE PARABOLIC MIRROR METHOD

1. If you have a flashlight that can be dismantled, or a soda can, you have a parabolic mirror. And if you have a parabolic mirror, you'll have fire soon enough.

2. If you're using a flashlight, unscrew the end and pull out the curved lens behind the light bulb. If you're using a soda can, cut the bottom (curved) end off of the can.

3. Place your parabolic mirror in the sun until a white spot of concentrated light forms in the center. Make sure it's positioned as a bowl, not a dome.

4. Place your tinder right on that spot and wait for the smoke and glow. Once those occur, blow to cause the fire to catch and begin adding your kindling.

5. You may have to build your tinder up a few inches high. The deeper the bowl, the closer the focus point will be to the ground. The shallower the bowl, the higher the focus point will be above the parabolic dish. For the shallow soda can bowl, the focus point will be a few inches in the air.

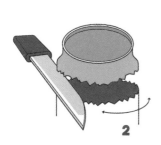

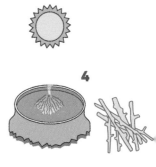

THE WATER BOTTLE METHOD

1. You'll need a smooth, clear, plastic water bottle with a dome-shaped top as well as plenty of patience.

2. Fill the bottle with water and try to knock all the bubbles out of it.

3. With the cap securely fastened, turn it upside down.

4. Drive two sticks in the ground to create a standing X and use it as a stand for the bottom of the water bottle. Position the water bottle so that the cap is touching the ground.

5. Look to see where the sunlight is being concentrated and place your dark, high quality tinder there.

6. Make sure the bottle is perfectly still.

7. Wait. Wait. Wait. Wait. Then maybe wait a little more.

8. When you see smoke and a glow, blow on it and prepare to light your kindling.

TYPES OF IGNITION
CONTINUED

THE BATTERY METHOD

A NINE-VOLT BATTERY and some steel wool make an excellent ignition source. All you have to do is allow the steel wool to come in contact with both battery leads at the same time. You will instantly see smoke and glowing red fibers.

You will need:
- A 9v battery
- Steel wool
- Tinder

1. Make sure you place the steel wool where you want to build your fire. Place the battery leads up against the wool. If need be, lightly brush the battery back and forth along the wool fibers.

2. When it starts to glow and smoke, gently blow on it until it ignites. Place the wool under your kindling and allow gaps to channel the air through as you place the kindling into the most efficient arrangement for growing the fire. You will need to add fresh kindling three or four times until the fire is sustainable enough to add a large piece of wood for long-burning fuel.

THE FLAT MIRROR METHOD

MIRRORS ARE incredibly powerful when it comes to focusing light but also dangerous for the same reasons. If left unattended, this method has the potential to start unwanted fires and/or kill wildlife. Be especially responsible and take the necessary safety precautions for yourself and your environment with this one.

You will need:
- 10-15 mirrors, each of which is 1-inch square or larger
- Sunlight
- Tinder

1. Make sure that your tinder is of the highest quality you can find (driest, darkest and most flammable). If the day is windy, stake your tinder to the ground, but do not adjust it with your hands once the mirrors have been placed.

2. Position all the mirrors in a curved arc around the tinder to reflect direct sunlight onto the exact same spot. Keep yourself and your clothing away from the focused sunlight in order to avoid serious burns. Stay behind the mirrors, wait for the smoke and glow and then carefully blow on the embers to ignite the fire

3. Dismantle and remove the contraption once your fire is lit to avoid unwanted fires.

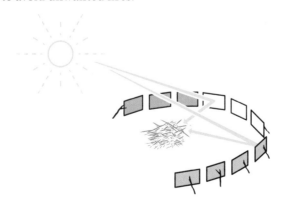

TYPES OF IGNITION
CONTINUED

THE FRICTION METHOD

THE OLD "rub two sticks together" method really does work, if you know what you're doing. You won't need much in the way of materials, just your stamina and patience. You can also fashion a bow drill to make things a little easier.

You will need:
- A flat piece of wood into which you will carve a notch
- A strong, dry stick
- Tinder
- A shoelace (for the bow drill, optional)
- A flexible stick (for the bow drill, optional)
- A chunk of wood (for the bow drill, optional)

1. Keep your tinder close by so that you can be ready to make it catch fire. Gouge a notch into the middle of the flat wood that will hold and stabilize the stick. Place one end of the stick in the notch of the flat piece of wood.

2. Hold the stick in between your palms and rub it briskly back and forth. The friction will eventually create smoke.

When you see a glow, place your tinder all around it and blow to make the fire catch.

3. You can also fashion a bow drill out of a flexible stick and a shoelace. On both ends of the bow, cut notches into each shoulder. Cut a notch into the center of the extra chunk of wood as well. Tie the ends of the shoelace in small loops and attach them to the bow by placing the loops into the shoulder notches. Wrap the taut shoelace once completely around the stick with the ends of the shoelace fastened securely to the shoulder notches of the bow. Place the end

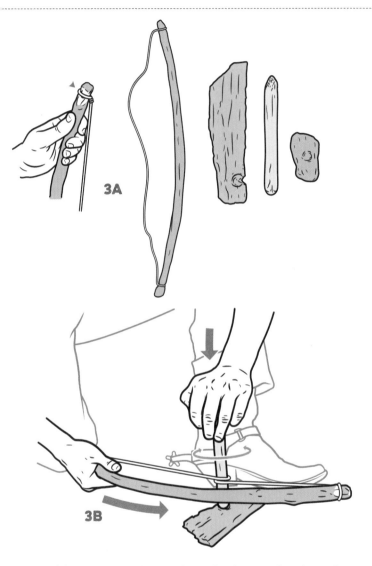

of the stick into the notch on the flat wood and use the notch in the separate chunk of wood to stabilize the top of the stick. Draw the bow back and forth in a sawing motion. This will twist the stick as it sits in the notch of the flat piece of wood, creating friction.

HOW TO **BUILD A TEEPEE FIRE**

ANY PEOPLE consider this fire their favorite as it is very easy to build. While it doesn't retain its shape for long once it really gets going, the initial channeling works well to get it started. Like the other fires, you can maintain this fire for as long as you can feed it.

You will need:
- A spark
- Tinder
- Kindling
- Logs

1. Pick a spot in a cleared area and lay your materials out around you.

2. Light your tinder on the ground. When it catches, begin to lay your sticks of kindling down. Once your kindling catches fire and burns reliably, take your logs and place them vertically around the base of the fire, leaning in toward the center and resting on each other at the top, teepee style.

3. As the fire burns, the logs will fall toward the center. This fire needs to be maintained and even reshaped from time to time. Eventually, you'll simply find yourself laying fresh logs straight down on the fire to keep it going. It will not look like a teepee in the end, but the initial shape did its job up front by allowing a high volume of air flow.

HOW TO
BUILD A
TOP-DOWN FIRE

OU CAN BUILD a fire in virtually any direction as long as you adhere to the basic principles. This fire is a good option when you want to do all the work up front and then let the fire go on its own for a while. It requires significantly less tending than a bottom-up fire.

You will need:
- A spark
- Tinder
- Kindling
- Wood

1. Place all your materials out and within easy reach. This allows you some economy of motion as you work.

2. Since this is a top-down fire, you need to build it "upside down." Start by laying your logs down in a squared-off pyramid. This means you will put your broadest pieces on the ground and use progressively smaller pieces as you build up.

3. On top of your wood, place your kindling. These small sticks should be together in one place but loose enough to allow air flow.

4. On top of everything, place your tinder. If you've already woven it into a bird's nest shape, good work, pilgrim. This will ensure it doesn't blow away.

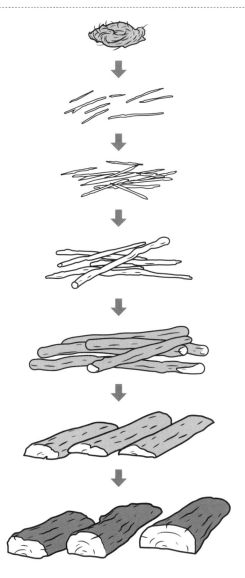

5. Choose your ignition source and throw your spark onto the tinder. Blow gently into it. It will burn down and catch the kindling, and the kindling will burn down and catch the wood.

HOW TO **BUILD A BOTTOM-UP FIRE**

 HIS STYLE OF fire is much more well-known and "traditional." You can build this one on a flat surface, in a pit, in a fireplace, in a grill, on a mound—almost anywhere. The one drawback is that it requires constant tending and frequent feeding. Always ensure you have a wide enough clearing for your intended fire size, watch it carefully and if need be, chase down blowing embers.

You will need:
- A spark
- Tinder
- Kindling
- Wood

1. Lay your materials around you to streamline your work.

2. Place your tinder on the ground and light it with your spark. When you are sure it will stay lit, add your kindling on top. You will need to keep adding more and more kindling until you have a good fire burning strong and consistently.

3. When you are confident your fire will not die, start adding your wood on top of the kindling. From this point on, as long as you want to maintain your fire, you will need to add wood. The upside is that all this wood is being converted into charcoal, which has many wilderness uses (pg. 134).

John Wayne sits at a campfire with some scouts during a visit to Meath School in the village of Ottershaw, Surrey, England, on October 28, 1960.

HOW TO **BUILD A STAR FIRE**

STAR FIRE is ideal if you want a very long-lasting fire to sleep by for warmth or protection. It requires about five good-sized logs, though, so be sure you have enough space.

You will need:
- A spark
- Tinder
- Kindling
- At least 5 good-sized logs

1. Ensure you have a wide clearing to avoid the risk of catching anything on fire accidentally.

2. Place all the logs in a star configuration with one end of each log coming together in a small circle in the middle.

3. Light your tinder and kindling in the center of the circle of logs. Tend and feed the fire until it burns bright and hot.

4. Push the end of each log into the fire and allow the logs to catch and burn. Over time, feed the fire by pushing each log closer in. This fire will produce a lot of charcoal. If you need to douse the fire prematurely, pull the logs out of the flames.

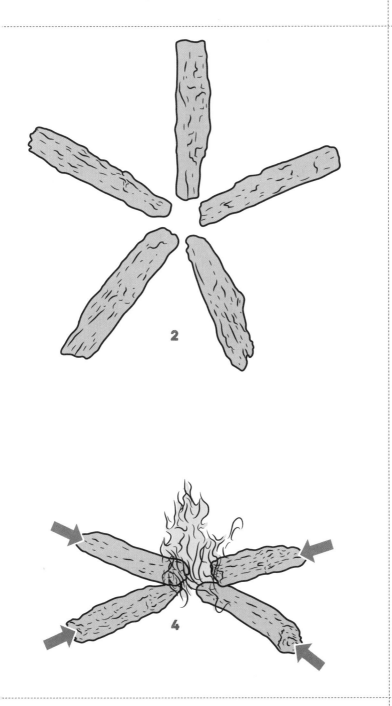

2

4

HOW TO
BUILD A LOG CABIN FIRE

 LOG CABIN fire is exactly what it suggests, except unlike a real log cabin, the seams between the logs are not sealed but rather left open to channel the air flow needed to feed the fire. And instead of a big open room in the center of your log cabin, you'll add a center "wall."

You will need:
- A spark
- Tinder
- Kindling
- At least 9 similarly-sized logs

1. Start by laying three logs parallel to each other, about 6 inches apart. For the sake of explanation, we will say the first three are laid out north/south. Lay three more logs perpendicular to and on top of the first three, making a layered square. These three are oriented east/west. On top of that layer, add three more logs oriented north/south. As long as it is structurally sound, this is usually enough to get started.

2. On top and in the middle of your cabin, light your tinder and kindling. The log walls of the cabin will take hours to be consumed by the fire. You can continuously build your walls as long as you want to maintain this fire.

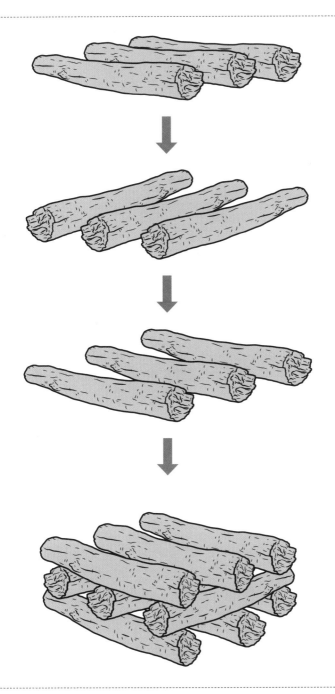

HOW TO
BUILD A DAKOTA HOLE FIRE

 HIS FIRE REQUIRES a bit of work, but it has some distinct advantages: You can keep your heat signature concealed; you can leave the fire unattended for a while and come back to it; it's completely shielded from the wind and partially from the rain and best of all, it's great for cooking.

You will need:
- A shovel or other digging implement
- A spark
- Tinder
- Kindling
- Logs

1. Start by digging a 2-foot deep hole and give it a generous diameter.

2. Dig an underground channel leading from the bottom of the fire pit back up to the surface several feet away from your hole. This acts as a chimney and channels air to feed the fire.

3. Light your tinder and kindling in the large, deep hole and bring the fire to a steady blaze.

4. Add your logs and ensure they are really burning. Since earth is moist and will therefore not burn, you can leave this fire for a while. This is a good time to build a shelter

(pgs. 138-169) or procure some fish or meat (pgs. 58-101) to cook. Just make sure there is nothing light like cardboard in the fire that could be caught by a gust of wind and blown out of the hole.

HOW TO BUILD A KEYHOLE FIRE

 HIS FIRE is ideal for cooking food directly in a bed of hot coals. It provides a containment area and becomes an in-ground oven.

You will need:
- A spark
- Tinder
- Kindling
- Logs
- A shovel or other digging implement
- A raking implement

1. Start by digging a round hole about a foot deep. Connected to that round hole, dig a rectangular channel about 18 inches long and 8 inches wide. This should resemble a keyhole.

2. You can build any style of fire you like here, but a teepee fire built in the round part of your keyhole often works particularly well.

3. Once you have a fire blazing, it will start to produce charcoal briquettes. Rake the charcoal over from the fire and into the rectangular channel. When you have plenty of hot coals, you can put your meal in the coals to cook. Maintain the main fire for warmth and to continually produce more hot coals. Keep raking the coals into the channel until you have enough to fully cook the food.

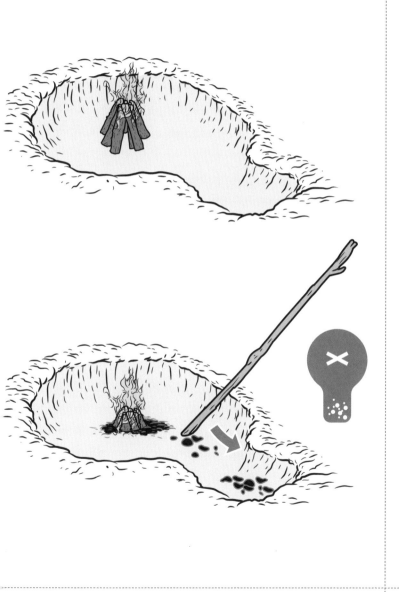

HOW TO **BUILD A SWEDISH STOVE FIRE**

HIS FIRE is specifically designed for cooking, and it gives you a flat surface to boot. It uses only one whole log, so this is a good option if wood is scarce.

You will need:
- A spark
- Tinder
- Kindling
- A dry, whole log
- An axe, hatchet, chain or other splitting implement

1. Take a whole log with two flat ends and split it lengthwise into four segments. These should be as uniform in size as possible.

2. Stand the split log on end and assemble it as if it were still whole.

3. Take your tinder and gently stuff it into the log at the center where the four points meet. Do not overstuff it as it still needs air flow.

4. Light the tinder. Once the tinder is lit, start adding small pieces of kindling and make sure each one catches on fire.

5. Eventually, the center parts of the log will catch on fire too. Continue to feed it tinder until you can see that the log itself is glowing. The splits allow for air flow, and you can cook food by placing a frying pan or a pot on top.

NOTE Make sure you choose a dry log. A wet one will smoke but not burn. You can split the log all the way down and assemble it to make a stove, but if you have the ability, it works best if you leave the bottom few inches intact. This will help you manage the fire as you go along. It is structurally more sound and even moveable.

HOW TO **BUILD A LEAN-TO FIRE**

 LEAN-TO FIRE is a good option if you happen to have one good-sized log and lots of kindling. This fire works well in windy conditions because the log itself is a natural windbreak.

You will need:
- A large log
- Tinder
- Lots of kindling
- A spark

1. Lay your log on the ground in a spot where the earth around it will not catch fire.

2. Place your tinder next to the log. Make sure it is nestled up nice and close.

3. Lay your kindling across the tinder with one end resting on the log and the other resting on the ground. You should see a lean-to shape.

4. Light the tinder under the kindling. It will take some time for the log to catch, so be generous with the amount of kindling you use.

HOW TO BUILD A WHOLE LOG FIRE

 HIS IS A BIT of a misnomer as this fire actually requires two whole (uncut and cylindrical) logs the entire time. The advantage of this fire is that with two whole logs, it will burn and burn and burn.

You will need:
- 2 whole, good-sized logs
- Tinder
- Kindling
- A spark

1. Align your logs parallel to each other and about a foot apart.

2. Place your tinder midway between the two logs and light it.

3. Add your kindling until you get a nice blaze going. This should eventually catch the middle of each log on fire.

4. The logs will begin to burn from the middle along the inside walls. As they burn, you can push the ends together to keep the fire fed—just make sure not to suffocate the fire as you do so. This fire will burn all the way to the end of both logs.

5. This type of fire can make a good cooking platform. You can place a grate, a griddle or a spit resting on both logs directly over the hottest spot and cook like a cowboy camping under the stars.

REFLECTING AND DIRECTING HEAT

 OW THAT YOU have so many options for fires, you'll want to know how to maximize the subsequent heat for warming and drying.

You will need one of the following:
- An emergency blanket (a.k.a. space blanket, Mylar blanket, thermal blanket) or any stretchable, reflective material
- A large rock, boulder or cave wall
- Bricks or sizable rocks
- A log wall
- Lots of wet earth and mud

1. If you will want to direct the heat, you can build your fire against a wood or stone wall. This can be a boulder, a cave or a wall you constructed from the stones, logs or earth and mud around you. NOTE: Keep air flow in mind as you decide on the exact position and materials. You want to direct the heat but not suffocate the flames.

2. Do not build the fire right up against the wall, but rather a couple feet in front of it. The wall will direct the heat away from it.

3. If you have an emergency blanket or any other reflective material, you can stretch that out behind your fire and attach it vertically at its four corners, two to trees or rocks

and two to the earth. This will reflect the heat and light from the fire back toward you.

NOTE Be very careful when using stones. Never take stones from water to use for fire as they can explode and throw shrapnel everywhere. Do not build your fire inside a cave with a low ceiling for the same reason. The ceiling can expand and chunks of rock can fall, putting you in danger. Use the outside wall of a cave to reflect your fire.

USES FOR CHARCOAL

 EYOND KEEPING you warm, cooking your food and sending signals, the fires you build will also produce a very useful material: charcoal. This black carbon residue is the result of wood being burned in an environment with low oxygen, and it can be used for everything from hunting to treating wounds. So rather than disposing of it once your fire is finished, keep some cooled charcoal on hand—you just might need it later.

To keep your charcoal intact for later use, you'll want to keep it away from moisture. If possible, store it in a metal container with a tight lid. The less porous the container the better, as you don't want any air getting in.

1. *CAMOUFLAGE*
If you're looking for an added advantage while hunting your next meal, charcoal can help you hide from your prey. You can use charcoal as camouflage by rubbing it on the exposed parts of your skin until you blend in better with your surroundings. This also prevents the sun from reflecting off your skin, making you less noticeable to animals you're approaching.

2. *TAKING NOTES*
If you need to make note of something or write a message to someone to signal for help but don't have a writing utensil, look no further than charcoal. It can be used to write on paper, if you have it, or anything in the wild from rocks to tree bark.

Above: Aldo Ray and John Wayne in *The Green Berets* (1968).

3. *FIRST AID*

If you're dealing with skin irritations such as bug bites, charcoal can be used as a topical application for quick relief. Additionally, charcoal can also be used to prevent poisoning. If you believe you may have ingested poison, quickly create a mixture of charcoal and clean drinking water and consume it. The charcoal will absorb the poison in your body.

HOW TO
EXTINGUISH
A FIRE

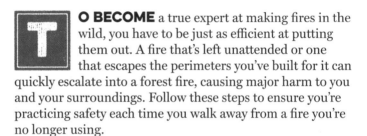

O BECOME a true expert at making fires in the wild, you have to be just as efficient at putting them out. A fire that's left unattended or one that escapes the perimeters you've built for it can quickly escalate into a forest fire, causing major harm to you and your surroundings. Follow these steps to ensure you're practicing safety each time you walk away from a fire you're no longer using.

1. You'll need plenty of water to be sure you've fully extinguished a fire. Fill a bucket or other carrying vessel with water and pour it evenly over the entire fire. Repeat as necessary to drown the fire.

2. Using a shovel or a long sturdy stick, mix the ashes and embers into the dirt and soil on the ground. Scrape all burned firewood and sticks to remove any clinging embers. Once those embers are loose, stir them up to make sure they get wet.

3. Carefully use your hand to feel the coals, embers and burned firewood to make sure all are cool to the touch. Double-check there are no lingering embers that are still burning.

4. Once you've confirmed everything has cooled down, pour more water onto the former fire. You can never be too safe, pilgrim.

John Wayne in *Hellfighters* (1968). The film shot on locations in Casper and Jackson Hole, Wyoming, and Midland, Baytown and Houston, Texas.

5. Check the surrounding area for any embers that may have floated and landed away from the fire. Look on the ground, in and around your shelter and on any or under any surface that could be concealing an ember.

John Wayne and Marceline Day in *The Telegraph Trail* (1933). The film included footage from Ken Maynard's Western *The Red Raiders* (1927).

CONSTRUCTING SHELTER

EVEN WHEN YOU'RE
OUT IN THE WILD, YOU
STILL NEED A PLACE
TO HANG YOUR HAT.

SHELTER TIPS AND OTHER CONSIDERATIONS

THERE ARE MANY THINGS you should consider before constructing a shelter.

• How much time and effort will be required?
• Do I have the time and energy?
• Will it adequately protect me?
• Do I have the tools I need or can I make them myself?
• Do I have enough materials?
• Can I modify an existing structure or natural shelter?

When it comes to selecting a shelter site, you will need to ask yourself:

• Is the space big enough for me to lie down?
• Is the ground level?
• Is it close to a signaling site?
• Is it close to a water source?
• Is it free from bugs and snakes?
• Is there protection from wild animals, falling rocks, trees and limbs?
• Can this site flood?
• Is there any danger from rising water, running water or avalanches?
• Can I make a fire close enough to keep me dry and warm?

Once you have evaluated your circumstances and environment accordingly, keep these tips in mind when constructing your shelter:

1. Only make your shelter as large as it needs to be. Your body will warm a small space.

2. Digging a runoff channel will help keep you dry.

3. A lean-to is the best choice of natural shelter. enough to keep you warm and dry, but far enough away not to catch your shelter on fire.

4. Choose a natural windbreak or create one.

5. Cold ground conducts heat away from your body. Pad your sleeping space with leaves, boughs, pine needles, moss or any other material you can collect. The rule of thumb is to build it up about 18 inches high.

6. When creating shingling for your shelter, lay the "tiles" in an overlapping fashion. This will ensure rainwater runs off of (rather than into) the shelter.

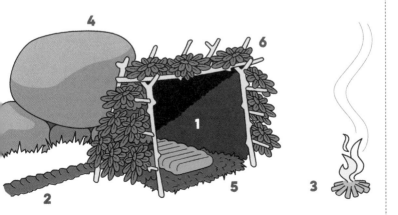

HOW TO CHOP DOWN A TREE WITH AN AXE

HILE TREES are great natural sources of shade and oxygen, they can often be more useful to us when they're no longer standing. This is especially true when you're building shelter in the wilderness. Whether you need a tree's materials or you just need to clear space for your shelter construction, you can use your axe to chop it down. Before you go swinging for the fences, read through these guidelines to make sure your chopping technique is safe and efficient.

1. The first thing to consider before making any moves toward cutting down a tree is whether or not you can do so safely. If the tree you're eyeing leans in one particular direction, that's where it will fall, so make sure its path is clear. To determine the distance of clear space you'll need, you can use the axe method: Hold your axe handle vertically at arm's length and look at it with one eye. Walk either toward or away from the tree until the top of the axe is aligned with the treetop and the bottom of the handle is aligned with the base of the tree. You can estimate that the tree will extend to roughly the point where your feet are once it falls, but you'll still want to allow for some extra room beyond that point to be on the safe side. You'll also want to make note of any large, dead branches resting on the tree limbs that could fall off and injure you on their way

John Wayne in *Allegheny Uprising* (1939). The film's working titles were *Pennsylvania Uprising*, *The First Rebel* and *Allegheny Frontier*.

HOW TO CHOP DOWN A TREE WITH AN AXE CONTINUED

down. If you're able to reach any, clear them off as best you can.

2. Once you've found the tree you'd like to take down and you're sure it's safe to do so, take your axe and begin cutting near the base of the tree facing the direction you want the tree to fall. You don't want to cut straight on—instead, you should be cutting at a downward angle. Keep going until you chop through about a third of the tree's diameter.

3. On the other side of the tree trunk, start a new cut about a foot or so higher than your original cut on the side from which you began. The goal is to create a wedge on either side of the tree, with a pillar of wood remaining in the middle acting as a hinge. Continue cutting until you're about halfway through the diameter of the tree, then return to the side where you made your original cut.

4. With your axe at the original cut, begin cutting at an upward angle toward the wedge on the other side of the tree. At this point, you'll want to pay close attention as the tree is ready to fall. While you may be expecting it to fall slowly while making plenty of noise, the reality is that it can happen quite swiftly and quietly without much warning. Once the tree begins to fall, run as fast as you can in the opposite direction.

SPOTTING A SICK TREE

Sometimes a tree needs to be chopped down simply for the sake of safety. If you're setting up camp in an area hosting what looks to be an unhealthy tree that's at risk of falling

John Wayne in
Sagebrush Trail
(1933).

on its own, it might be in your best interest to take it down yourself before it falls on you or the shelter you've built.

If the tree is heavily leaning to one side rather than standing up straight, it could be decaying. You can also tell by looking at the branches—if they seem to be only loosely connected to the trunk, that's another possible indicator that the tree is not well. For a closer assessment of the tree's health, you can scratch a small portion of bark off the tree and observe the wood underneath. If it's a vibrant green, then the tree is doing well. If the wood is black, however, consider grabbing your axe and chopping the tree down to avoid a potential disaster.

TIPS FOR
HANGING A HAMMOCK

F YOU HAPPENED to pack a hammock before heading out on your journey, good move, pilgrim. Though you may already be a pro at setting up this sleeping system on your front porch or in your backyard at home, it's a somewhat different experience out in the wild. Here's how to hang your hammock so that it's safe, comfortable and not a burden on your environment.

1. When choosing your hammocking trees, make sure they don't show any signs of decay (pg. 144). You'll want to find trees that are thick and sturdy, at least 6 inches in diameter. And since you obviously can't move two trees to be the perfect distance apart, you might have to do some trial and error to find a good fit. Keep in mind that if the trees are too close together, your hammock will sag to the ground; if they're too far apart, your hammock will be too taut and more likely to flip.

2. Most hammocks will come with the materials you need for suspending, such as straps, paracord and carabiners. If yours doesn't, you can use common rope and hang your hammock using a figure-eight knot on each tree (pg. 44).

3. Once your hammock is set up, sit and lay in different positions to test it out. The center should be no more than 18 inches off the ground, while the strap sides should be slanting at about 30 degrees above the ground.

John Wayne relaxes in a hammock, c. 1950s.

Ultimately, though, you just want to be comfortable and assured that the hammock is sturdy, so make adjustments accordingly.

HOW TO **BUILD A RAISED BED**

 HO SAYS you can't have a little luxury while sleeping in the great outdoors? Though some of the shelters you might build will not allow much space for a raised bed, this can be a good option for the likes of a tarp shelter (pg. 152) or a teepee shelter (pg. 162). Or, you might just want to use it as an extra piece of furniture to rest on at your site during the day.

You will need:
- 2 sturdy logs, at least 4 inches in diameter
- 4 to 6 thick, straight sticks about 2 feet longer than the length of your body (to be used as slats)
- 4 sturdy sticks (to be used as stakes)

1. The pair of logs will serve as the head and foot of your bed and will be used to support the slats. To determine how far apart your logs should be, lay down on the ground with your arms outstretched above your head. The "head" log should go where your hands, and the "foot" should be placed parallel to it, at your feet.

2. The number of slats you use will depend on the size of your body. As you lay them out vertically, bridging the two logs, they should extend beyond the head and foot logs by about 6 inches on each side. To determine the spacing between slats, leave about 2 to 4 finger widths between each. While it may seem wise to arrange them as close together as possible, leaving some room will actually be more comfortable as it allows you to sleep

on your side without your hip bone being right up against the wood.

3. Now you'll want to secure the outermost slats so that they don't roll off the logs as you sleep. Take your four sturdy sticks and position one at each corner of the bed vertically, so that they're touching the outer slats. Carefully hammer (pg. 22) each one into the ground as you would a stake, just enough so that they don't wiggle around in the ground and are sticking out enough to hold the slats in place.

4. The inner slats should remain loose so you can adjust them as needed. If you have a sleeping bag or a blanket, place it on top of the bed for added comfort.

HOW TO **BUILD A PONCHO SHELTER**

PONCHO AND its liner are the Green Beret's best friend. Poncho liners frequently come in handy in the wilderness—they can be used to carry water, make shelter, make seats, waterproof other items, make a raft, keep warm, camouflage and much more.

You will need:
- A poncho liner
- Lashing
- 4 stakes
- A large, fallen tree

1. For a flat shelter designed solely to create shade, lay your poncho liner on the ground in a big square. If the corners do not have grommets, you can take a rock or a small clump of earth, place it on the material about 6 inches in from the corner, wrap the material closed around it and tie it off with your lashing. This provides a place to anchor from and allows you to put some tension on it. If the corners have grommets, tie your lashings through them and leave a generous amount of tail to tie off to your anchor point.

2. Choose four trees, rocks or some combination of both and use those to anchor all four corners. If you simply want shade, you can tie the entire liner level with the ground.

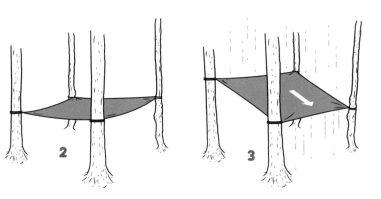

3. If you are sheltering from rain or snow, you'll want to do things differently. Stretch your poncho liner out between your four anchor points and tie each one as high up in the air as you want it to be, creating a slant for runoff. A taut line hitch (pg. 50) will be your best knot for taking in any slack.

4. For an alternative shelter from precipitation, take a long section of lashing and tie it taut between two trees. Take your poncho liner and drape it over the taut line. If you want it very close to the ground, you can place the line right down the middle of your poncho liner and create a makeshift pup tent. If you want it a little higher or you have a sizable fallen tree to use as a wall, you can drape most of the poncho liner on one side of the taut line. Run the line lengthwise along the fallen tree and drape the liner from the felled tree to the ground. Just leave about 6 to 8 inches of it bent over the line and overlapping the tree. Stake all four corners to the ground. Two stakes will be in front of the tree and two stakes will be behind it.

HOW TO **BUILD A TARP SHELTER**

TARP IS VERSATILE like a poncho liner but with a couple differences. Tarps are generally bigger and have no hole and hood in the center. If the edges and corners of your tarp have no grommets, you can use the same rock and earth technique as you did with the poncho liner to give you a place from which to tie them down and tension them.

You will need:
- A tarp
- 6 stakes
- Lashing
- 2 sticks, each about 4 feet long (optional, if lashing/trees are not available)

1. You can make a tent with some ground cover from a single tarp. You will need to place ⅓ of it on the ground and use ⅓ of it for the tent walls. Place the first third of the tarp on the ground and stake it down in four corners.

2. Using your lashing, tie a taut line a few feet in the air between two trees, lengthwise down the center of your ground portion

3. Being careful not to disturb the stakes, fold the remaining portion in half over your taut line and stake down the edges. Make sure the final piece overlaps the ground portion of the tarp so you don't get wind or rain in your tent.

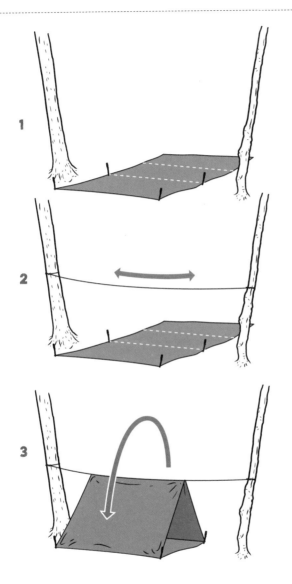

NOTE If you do not have trees and/or lashing, you can still use a tarp. Instead of hanging it over a taut line, prop it up from the inside with your 4-foot sticks. Make sure not to poke unnecessary holes in the material.

HOW TO **BUILD A DEBRIS HUT**

THIS SHELTER is like John Wayne's Best Actor Academy Award—it requires a bit of time and effort, but it's certainly well worth it. And while it is rudimentary, the debris hut remains a favorite shelter among Green Berets because of its camouflage capability.

You will need:
- A bifurcated tree (a tree that forks in two directions)
- A 10 to 15-foot long sapling or felled tree
- Many tree limbs, sticks and branches
- Pine boughs
- Sod or moss
- Tree barks
- Leaves

1. Find a bifurcated tree with the split occurring about 3 to 4 feet from the ground. Drag your sapling or small, felled tree and drop one end into the Y of the bifurcated tree. The other end will be on the ground resulting in a sloping support beam.

2. Collect as many fresh, soft pine boughs as you can find and lay them down on the ground under the support beam. This will be your bed. Ideally, you want it to be 18 to 24 inches thick to keep you warm and dry all night.

3. Take your branches and tree limbs and begin the process of building your walls. You will use the tallest ones closest to the bifurcated tree and the shortest ones farthest away. Lay them side by side with the upper end resting against

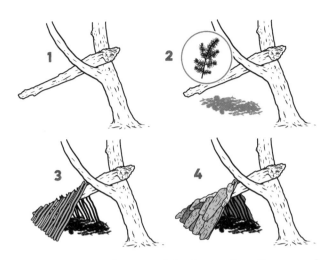

your support beam and the low end on the ground.
Building both walls should result in an A frame around
your bedding.

4. Once you have walls, you will need to waterproof them.
You can use sod, moss or tree bark to accomplish this.
Cut your material into the largest pieces possible. Start
at the bottom of your walls on the outside of your hut
and begin to lay your "shingles" from the ground up.
Lay them out along the entire length of wall along
the ground and then start on your second row. Each
successive row should overlap the row beneath it so
any precipitation runs off instead of running inside
your shelter.

5. When you've covered the entire outside of your hut
with shingles, you can fill in any gaps with leaves.
Leaves also help to break up the silhouette and make
your hut harder to spot.

NOTE Making the shelter as small as possible is
advantageous not only because it requires fewer materials
and less time, but also because a small space is easier to
keep warm with your body heat.

HOW TO **BUILD A SNOW CAVE**

 N TENTH SPECIAL Forces Group Winter Environmental Training, Green Berets learn that a single candle in a well-made snow cave can bring the temperature up to about 50 degrees Fahrenheit. While you don't want your cave to be drafty, you do need to make sure you have sufficient ventilation—especially while you sleep, or else you can asphyxiate. Make sure you have deep snow and are not in an area with any risk of avalanches. If you can't find the right conditions, just dig a trench and lay down in it for partial shelter. A snow cave is going to take hours to be built correctly. Rest when you need to. Move slowly. Do not overexert or overheat. Stay hydrated.

You will need:
- A digging implement
- A candle (optional)

1. Select your snowy site and check to make sure the depth is at least 6 feet of snow. Pack it down tightly with your hands, feet and body weight. Allow it to cool and harden for about 2 hours.

2. Choose which side is best suited for the entrance. Slowly and methodically, begin digging a tunnel wide enough to crawl through. You will want to leave at least 24 inches of snow for your walls and ceiling. You can help yourself by measuring the thickness on the outside and sticking something like a 2-foot long branch into the snow, which will tell you to stop digging when you reach it.

3. Hollow out the dome of your cave slowly and carefully.

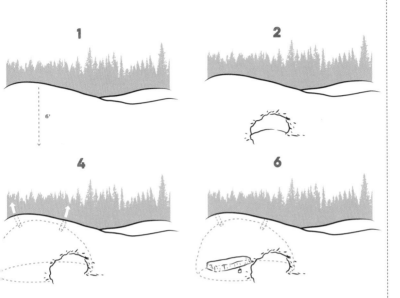

You do not want to cause a cave in. If you can, slope the entrance up and make the floor inside your cave higher than your entrance to reduce draft and retain heat.

4. Drill two small, angled holes in opposite sides of the ceiling for ventilation.

5. Rub the inside walls and ceiling smooth to prevent dripping as the snow melts.

6. On the floor, use the snow to form a 6-inch high shelf to use for a bed. Then, add any insulating material you have on hand for more comfortable bedding.

7. Mark the outer perimeter of the cave and do not walk or step on the cave from the outside.

8. While you are inside the cave, you can keep a candle burning for warmth if you have one. Your own body heat will also help raise the temperature. Seal the entrance with snow before you sleep.

HOW TO **BUILD A DESERT PIT SHELTER**

 F YOU HAVE a tarp or a poncho liner, you can build a very expedient desert shelter. However, be sure to consider the dry heat and the sun as you work. Make sure to take plenty of breaks, rest and hydrate to avoid sustaining a heat injury.

You will need:
- A tarp, poncho liner or large piece of material
- A digging implement
- Good-sized rocks, or lashing and stakes

1. Dig a shallow trench large enough for you to lie down in comfortably with all of your body below ground level. The trench should have sloping ramps at the head and foot to help with ventilation. If you have the option to choose a shaded area, do so. If you have the option to choose the direction in which your trench is oriented, put the head end directly into the wind.

2. Stretch your material out over the trench and either stake down the corners or line all the edges with heavy rocks. Since rain is not usually a problem in the desert, you're primarily seeking shelter from the sun.

3. When you're lying down in your trench under your tarp, you should feel a draft with the breeze. The combination of shade and evaporative cooling from the draft should help you stay hydrated and safe from a heat injury.

Pedro Armendáriz and John Wayne in *3 Godfathers* (1948). The film shot on location in Death Valley, Califonia.

HOW TO **BUILD A LEAN-TO SHELTER**

 **HE LEAN-TO** is among the quickest and easiest shelters to construct if you encounter the right circumstances. If you're able to find a sizable fallen tree, you're basically only building half a shelter.

You will need:
- A fallen tree
- Good-sized sticks, limbs or branches
- A poncho liner
- Stakes

1. Upon finding your fallen tree, gather your sticks to make the remaining wall. Place the sticks against the tree at a 45 degree angle as shown in the illustration. You should immediately see the lean-to shape.

2. Cover the wall you created with your poncho liner and stake down the corners.

3. Add pine boughs, leaves or some other soft material for your bed. If you have an emergency mylar blanket you can use it as a ground cloth or you can wrap yourself up in it to stay warm.

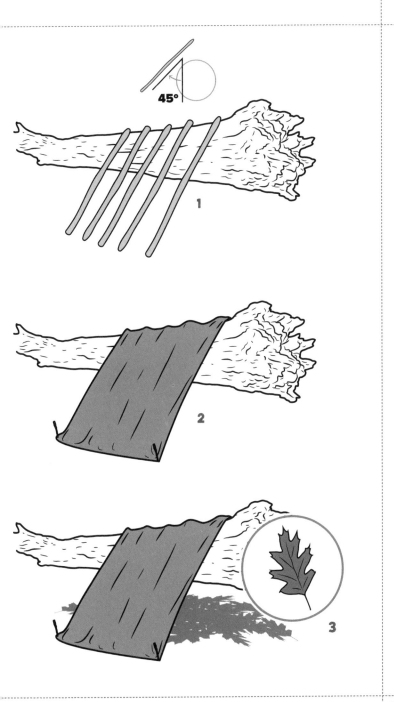

HOW TO **BUILD A TEEPEE SHELTER**

 HIS STYLE of shelter works well if you don't have much time to build or if you want something you can sit up inside of. Quick and comfortable, who could complain?

You will need:
- 6 tall branches or saplings to act as your support posts
- A tarp
- Stakes
- Lashing

1. Choose a site to accommodate your intended shelter. Around a circle of approximately 5 feet in diameter, drive your six evenly-spaced saplings as deep into the ground as you can. They should be green enough to be slightly flexible. Once they are planted in the ground, join them together at the top in the center of the circle and lash them together. This is your frame.

2. Take your tarp and wrap it around the outside of the frame. It will be narrow at the top and wide at the bottom. Lash the tarp to the gathered tops of the saplings. Stake the bottom of the tarp to or at each of the saplings at the ground.

3. Your entrance is where the ends of tarp come together. Fold the flap back to enter or exit.

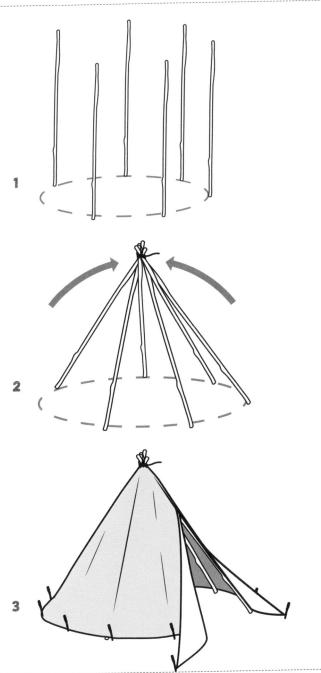

1

2

3

HOW TO BUILD A GREENHOUSE SHELTER

 GREENHOUSE'S FUNCTION is to intensify the heat of the sun. That is the general idea here as well.

You will need:
- A large, clear, plastic tarp
- Pine boughs (to create a bed 18 to 24 inches thick)
- 4 tall green saplings
- Lashing

1. Arrange your pine boughs in the sun stacked in rows, about 18 to 24 inches thick.

2. Drive your four saplings into the ground as deeply as you can around the four corners of your bed. Bend each one toward the center of the bed and lash them together.

3. Cover the whole structure with a sheet of clear plastic tarp. Cut two small ventilation holes in the top of the tarp.

4. Allow the heat of the sun to raise the temperature inside your greenhouse. It should be warmer than the ambient air when you go to bed, and the plastic will trap your body heat.

5. You can also open this shelter on one side and build a fire a few feet away. The back and side walls of plastic will retain and reflect the heat back to you in your bed. Again, the smaller the shelter, the more efficiently it will heat.

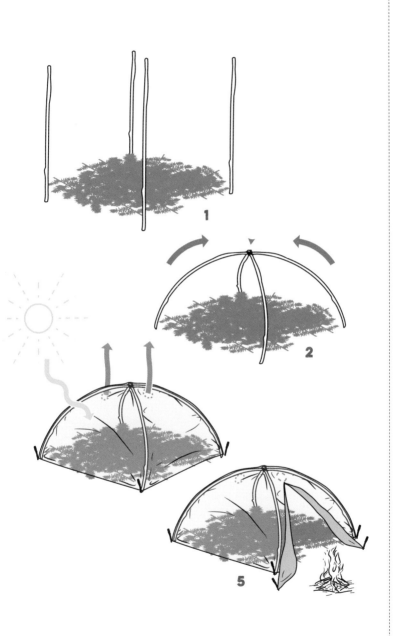

1

2

5

HOW TO **MAKE A VISUAL PERIMETER ALARM**

OHN WAYNE would never allow a foe to sneak up on him—especially while he was resting or cooking a hard-earned meal. A visual perimeter alarm can silently alert you when someone or something has come too close to your shelter.

You will need:
- At least 2 mini glow sticks
- A mouse trap
- Lashing

1. Test your alarm first on a throwaway glow stick to see if the trap has enough power to activate it. Lash one mousetrap to a tree oriented in a direction you can see from your camp.

2. Place the glow stick in the trap. Set the spring of the trap and attach a line outward from there to another tree. When determining the correct height above ground, you will need to ascertain what predators are around and how big you can reasonably expect them to be.

3. When something trips the line, the trap will spring and activate the glow stick.

John Wayne takes a closer look in the World War II drama *Operation Pacific* (1951). The film sees the legend as Duke Gifford, a U.S. Navy Lt. Commander leading his submarine, the *Thunderfish*, on a rescue mission in the Pacific after taking aboard a group of nuns and orphans who traveled through 40 miles of jungle in hopes of reaching safety. The film shot on location in Hawaii, and the submarine used for outdoor sequences featuring the *Thunderfish* was an actual Navy submarine known as *Thunder*. A full-size replica of the vessel was built for interior shots.

HOW TO **MAKE AN AUDIBLE PERIMETER ALARM**

 N THE EVENT of an intruder, it's often advantageous to hear the threat before you see it. A perimeter alarm can be made with anything you have on hand that makes noise.

You will need:
- Lashing
- Empty soda cans, bottles, bells, hollow bamboo, empty coconuts or anything else you can scrounge

1. Tie three or four empty and partially crunched soda cans or glass bottles together in a cluster.

2. Run a continuous line low to the ground where it can be easily tripped. Attach your cluster of noise makers and place them out of sight if you can. For example you could put them in or behind a bush.

3. You can make as many of these as you want and place as many lines and clusters out as you have materials to make. Make sure that they dangle completely off the ground or they will fail to make much noise.

4. Anything that tugs on the line will make the alarm sound. Be sure to remember where you placed your lines so you do not trip or set off your own alarm.

John Wayne visits troops in Vietnam, c. 1960s. As the star's son Ethan Wayne recalls, the icon always had time for American heroes. One night when there was some commotion outside their home in Newport Harbor, Duke grabbed his gun to investigate. "It ended up being some soldiers who had just returned from overseas," Ethan says. The two men had taken a boat to their hero's home in the middle of the night. "Dad told them 'Come on up and have a drink with me,' and they talked for about a half hour before Dad sent them on their way," Ethan remembers.

John Wayne in *Island in the Sky* (1953). That year, Duke also co-produced the John Farrow film *Plunder of the Sun*.

MASTERING YOUR SURROUNDINGS

KNOWING YOUR
ENVIRONMENT WILL
HELP YOU OVERCOME
ITS OBSTACLES.

HOW TO **SEND RESCUE SIGNALS**

HE UNIVERSAL distress sign is anything that comes in threes: three fires, three columns of smoke, three blasts of a whistle, three flashes of light reflected from a signal mirror, three glow sticks, etc. A great way to get someone's attention is to do something visual or auditory three times.

You will need one of the following:
- A glow stick and a string, about 2 feet long
- A whistle (see pg. 26)
- Fire
- A signal mirror

1. Green Berets who are trying to signal from ground to air will make a "buzzsaw" of light. Tie a glow stick to a string about 2 feet long and whirl it around your head. You will make a 4-foot disc of light that can be seen by searching aircraft. If there are three people in your party and enough materials available, have everyone do this.

2. Blow three short, loud blasts on your whistle at regular intervals. Remember, you can whistle for far longer than you can shout.

3. Build three fires (pgs. 102-137) in a roughly triangular shape. Select a prominent spot so they can be seen from far away by passing aircraft. If it's daytime, choose fuel that will create a lot of smoke. A good rule to remember is the less flammable something is the more smoke it produces when burning. Wet things make great smoke.

John Wayne in *Island in the Sky* (1953). The radio used in the film was functional and based on a World War II German emergency transmitter.

4. Reflect the light off your signal mirror and aim it in the direction of help. If you see an aircraft, aim it right at them. You can do this by making a peace symbol with one hand and using that as your sight. Look through your sight at the target and flash the light between your fingers.

HOW TO
MAKE A MAP

 F YOU HAVE paper and pencil, you can create a map and take it with you. If not, you can make one in the dirt. While you cannot carry your dirt map with you, drawing it out will help you receive, process, assimilate and recall information about your surroundings.

1. Ascend to the highest place you can safely reach. This might mean climbing a mountain, a hill or a tree.

2. Take note of the terrain features.

3. Draw your map out in a way that makes sense to you. Try to orient it with north at the top for easy use. Remember, the sun rises in the east and sets in the west. This allows you to find north.

Here are some tips for orienting yourself as part of this technique:

• Choose what's known as a backstop—pick a non-changing terrain feature and use it to help you determine if you need to turn back (i.e. "If I reach that river, I've gone too far").

RIDGE LINES   **DRAWS**

SPURS

SADDLES

CLIFFS

FOREST

PRAIRIE

BODY OF WATER

SAND DUNES

DIRECTION OF THE SUN

THE WEATHER

HOW TO MAKE A MAP *continued*

• See if there's a good "handrail" along the way, such as a creek, river or ridge line. If so, draw it on your map so you have a feature you can follow along your route.

• Note any wetlands on your map and avoid heading into them. The thick growth of vegetation is hard to traverse.

• Keep the weather and its direction of movement in mind and note areas on your map where you can take shelter.

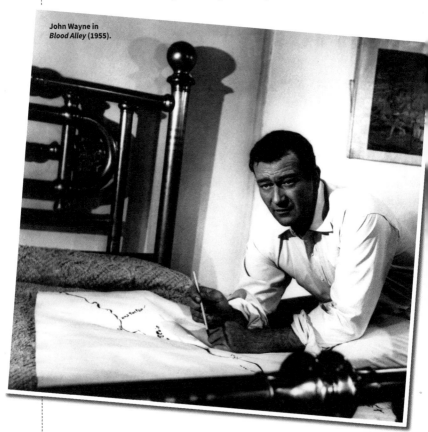

John Wayne in
Blood Alley (1955).

FINDING YOUR WAY

F YOU'RE HAVING trouble getting back on the ol' dusty trail, fear not—here's how you can craft your own compass.

1. Take a needle and stroke the end of it on a magnet or on silk. If you don't have either of those, you can use your hair or a piece of leather.

2. Suspend the magnetized needle from a piece of string or hair.

3. Hang the suspended needle inside a clear plastic or glass bottle to avoid it being disturbed by air currents.

The free-hanging magnetized needle will point north/south.

You also can use a paperclip, bobby pin, safety pin or any other thin piece of metal that can be magnetized. If you don't have the means to suspend it, you can float the needle on a leaf in the water. You will know you did it correctly if it automatically corrects its own orientation after you suspend or float it.

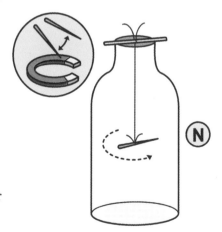

PACE COUNTING

OW CAN YOU MEASURE distance without any tools? By using your own two feet, pilgrim! Mastering this skill will give you a better sense of how far you've walked, which is a tremendous asset when combined with a map and a compass, and could potentially save your life when you're lost in the wild.

1. Measure out 100 yards, then designate the spot with a stick or some other marker so you can measure your pace against the same exact distance each time.

2. At a normal stride, walk the entire 100 yards, counting your paces. Note: Only measure your left footfall. Every time your left foot hits the ground, that counts as one pace. Record how many paces it takes you to cover 100 yards.

3. Do this three times to ensure you're consistent. You'll also need to do this on level ground as well as uphill and downhill, as there will be a difference between the three terrains.

Remember: Not all paces are the same. Everyone's pace varies according to their height and other measurements.

If you're worried about losing your place as you count multiple hundreds of yards in the wild, there are many systems you can use to keep track. For example, some people use the buttons on a button-down shirt (button or unbutton one with every 100 yards). You can also pick up a blade of grass every 100 yards, or make marks on your skin or gear. Use your noggin—you'll find that being able to measure distance without using tools can feel pretty empowering.

John Wayne in *Legend of the Lost* (1957). The film's exteriors were shot in Libya.

STAR-BASED NAVIGATION

N THE NORTHERN Hemisphere, we can count on one star to appear relatively unchanged all year long: the North Star. This star, also called Polaris or Pole Star, is not the biggest or the brightest but it is the one that never seems to move. Knowing how to identify it can help you navigate at night.

Depending on your hemisphere, you will need to be able to identify:
• The Big Dipper
• The Little Dipper
• The Southern Cross
• The Pointer Stars
• The moon at its one-quarter phase

1. The Big Dipper comprises seven stars. In the Northern Hemisphere, it is oriented so that the bowl of the spoon is facing up, as if in use. The Little Dipper appears above the Big Dipper, and it also comprises seven stars. The Little Dipper is considerably smaller than the Big Dipper and is poised upside down as if it's pouring something into the bowl of the Big Dipper. Once you identify the Little Dipper, you have found the North Star. The North Star is the very last star on the handle of the Little Dipper. You can navigate north according to that star.

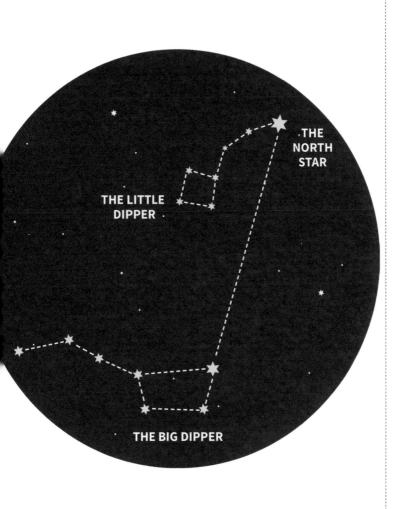

THE NORTH STAR

THE LITTLE DIPPER

THE BIG DIPPER

STAR-BASED NAVIGATION *continued*

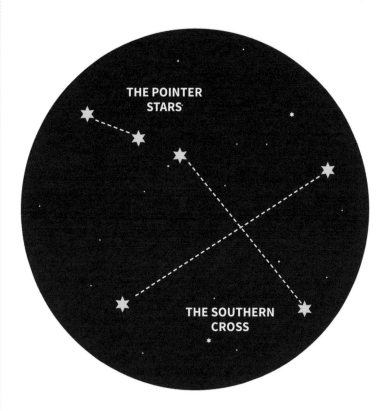

2. In the Southern Hemisphere there is a constellation called the Southern Cross. It appears as a cross in the sky, tilted to the left. Below and to the left of the Southern Cross are the Pointer Stars. There are two prominent Pointer Stars which are stacked on top of one another. If you draw an imaginary line through the long axis of the Southern Cross and another imaginary line straight out from between the two Pointer Stars, the place where those two imaginary lines meet is roughly south.

THE MOON AT ITS ONE-QUARTER PHASE

3. You can also navigate according to the moon when
it is at its quarter phase. Look at the quarter moon
and draw an imaginary line from the top horn to the
bottom horn, then extend that line all the way down
to the horizon. If you're in the Northern Hemisphere,
the place where that imaginary line touches Earth is
roughly south. If you are in the Southern Hemisphere,
the place where the imaginary line touches Earth is
roughly north.

NATURE-BASED NAVIGATION

 F YOU NEED to find your way on a cloudy day, you can use these clues from nature.

1. For every region there are prevailing winds (the normal direction wind blows from day to day). You can figure out the direction of the prevailing winds by standing facing into the blowing wind each day for a period of time.

2. Trees are not symmetrical. They are shaped by wind as they grow. Look for a tree in a clearing from all angles. Make sure to choose a tree with no wind break behind it, a tree that acts as a windbreak itself. The sparse side is upwind and the bushy side is downwind. If the wind is blowing from the west, the bushy side of the tree will be pointed east.

3. Likewise, trees grow best where they get the most direct sunlight. Knowing the sun rises in the east and sets in the west can help you figure out from which direction the tree gets the most sunlight. The healthiest and bushiest part of the tree will be the side that gets the lion's share of sunshine (usually the south side).

4. A spider's web can become a compass if you know which way the wind blows in your area. All spider webs are suspended, so if you know which way the prevailing winds are coming from, you can determine the four cardinal compass points when you observe the direction the web is blowing.

DEAD RECKONING

 EAD RECKONING is short for deduced reckoning. Having this skill can keep you oriented as you move from position to position. Green Berets use this skill when doing over-the-horizon movements in the desert and over water. It's an essential skill for long-range navigation.

You will need one of the following:
- A compass (pg. 177)
- A map (pg. 174)
- A watch
- An understanding of your current position

1. Mark your current position on your map.

2. Decide on a heading (the direction you wish to walk) and use your watch to note the time of your departure.

3. Use the compass to stay on track.

4. Keep track of your pace count (pg. 178).

5. When you stop, take a look at your map. By your pace count, you should know how far you traveled. Check to see how long it took you. On your map, you can plot your position by knowing where you were when you started, how far you moved and in which direction. Having a watch and a pace count provides the ability to measure distance.

FOR SAFETY'S SAKE, the best practice on every rappel style would be to have someone at the bottom on belay. That individual would watch the person on rappel with the rope in their hands and pull it tight with all their weight if the rappel turned into a fall, stopping the rappelling person in mid air.

SWISS RAPPELLING

WISS RAPPELLING was designed to accompany the Swiss seat harness (pg. 54) but can be done with commercial harnesses as well. This style does rely on a harness and carabiner to work.

You will need:
- A harness
- A climbing grade carabiner with a locking screw gate
- A climbing rope
- Anchor points, either solid trees or boulders
- Leather gloves

1. Anchor your rope with a figure-eight (pg. 44) backed up with a square knot (pg. 41) and toss it down the intended route, ensuring it reaches the bottom with rope to spare.

2. Put your harness on and attach the carabiner to the front through all the layers of rope or harness and with the locking screw gate facing up. The large axis should be facing away from you.

3. Put a little slack in the line above you. Put the rope through the screw gate (which is attached to you and facing up), wrap it once around the bottom of the carabiner and click it once more through the screw gate.

You should see a corkscrew of line only on the back spine of the carabiner and it should be wrapped once completely around.

4. Lock the screw gate and double check it. Put your leather gloves on.

5. Standing with your back to the route, hold the top end of the rope lightly in your non-dominant hand above the carabiner. This is your guide hand.

6. Pick up the slack end of the rope in your dominant hand and put that hand behind your back with your fist closed around the rope. This is your brake hand in the brake position.

7. Open your brake hand and straighten your elbow, allowing your arm to point out to the side by about 45 degrees. This is your position while in motion. Back over the ledge and put your weight on the rope. Bend at the waist into a 90 degree angle with your feet firmly on the rock. Let yourself down step by step. Close your brake hand and bring it into the small of your back to stop.

BELGIAN RAPPELLING

OR BELGIAN style rappelling, your anchor points, climbing rope, harness and carabiner will remain exactly the same as they were for Swiss rappelling. All that will change is where you run the rope on your body. Green Berets use this style when carrying a heavy pack because it helps to keep you upright and slows down the speed of your rappel.

You will need:
- A harness
- A climbing grade carabiner with a locking screw gate
- A climbing rope
- Anchor points, either solid trees or boulders
- Leather gloves

1. Set yourself up exactly as you did for Swiss rappelling with your climbing rope, anchor points, harness, gloves and carabiner.

2. Run the rope through the carabiner the same way.

3. Hold the top end of the rope lightly in your non-dominant hand above the carabiner. This is your guide hand. Run the slack end of the rope over your shoulder and across your back to the opposite hand. Pick it up by your waist in your dominant hand. This is your brake hand. You will want to hold the rope, palm up, with your arm extended out to the side.

4. Back over the ledge and put your weight on the rope. Bend at the waist into a 90 degree angle, feet firmly on the rock. Open your brake hand to let yourself down. Close it to stop.

SOUTH AFRICAN RAPPELLING

HIS IS ANOTHER style of emergency rappelling that requires nothing but a double rope and gloves.

You will need:
- A climbing rope more than double the length of your route (NOTE: A double rope can either be two ropes laid side by side or one rope doubled in half)
- Anchor points, either solid trees or boulders
- Leather gloves

1. Choose at least two anchor points and tie off your climbing rope using non-slip knots such as the bowline (pg. 40) or the figure-eight (pg. 44). Note: It's always a good idea to back up your non-slip knots with square knots (pg. 41). Drop the free-running end of the rope down the rappel route. Make sure the rope reaches past the bottom of the route.

2. Facing uphill, divide the rope into two sections and place one on each side of your body.

3. Wrap the sections of rope around your waist from back to front, mirror image to each other. Pass them through the front of your legs at the crotch.

4. Pick both ends up behind you with your dominant hand and bring that hand out to the side. This is your brake hand.

5. Back over the ledge and put your weight on the rope. Bend at the waist into a 90 degree angle with your feet firmly on the rock. Open your brake hand to let yourself down. Close it to stop.

AUSTRALIAN RAPPELLING

 PECIAL FORCES use this style of rappel to keep a usable weapon in one hand while in motion. To make it easier, you'll use a figure-eight belay device attached to your carabiner.

You will need:
- A harness
- A climbing grade carabiner with a locking screw gate
- A climbing rope
- Anchor points
- A figure-eight belay device
- Leather gloves

1. Set yourself up exactly as you did for Swiss and Belgian rappelling with your climbing rope, anchor points, harness, gloves and carabiner.

2. Run the rope through the figure-eight device attached to your carabiner instead of through the carabiner itself. Take a bight of rope and pass it through the large eye and over the neck of the small eye, then put the small eye onto the carabiner and lock the screw gate. Check the entire length of line and make sure you have a perfect U shape from the initial bight that went through the large eye all the way back to your anchor point. Double check it. Put your gloves on.

3. You are hooked to the line the same way as before but now you must turn around by 180 degrees and face downhill. Your brake hand is still your downhill hand but since your chest is facing downhill, you will need to

close your fist and bring it across your chest to brake.
Unlike the other styles, your non-dominant hand is free
on Australian rappel.

BODY RAPPELLING

 NLIKE THE OTHER styles, body rappelling puts you sideways to the route. This style should be reserved for easy, low-risk routes. It requires two ropes or one doubled rope but no harness or carabiner.

You will need:
- Two ropes, or a double length of rope for the intended route
- Anchor points
- Leather gloves

1. Tie your doubled climbing rope to your anchor points and drop the free running ends down the rappel route. Make sure the rope reaches past the bottom of the route.

2. Standing sideways to the route, run the rope horizontally across your back at the shoulder blade level. One arm will be uphill and one will be downhill.

3. Wrap the rope once around each arm in a loose corkscrew and keep the rope in both hands. The uphill hand has taut rope and the downhill hand has slack rope.

4. Lower yourself down sideways to the route, standing in a T with both arms held straight out to the sides. You can use both hands as brake hands. Make your way down in this position one step at a time.

HOW TO
RECOGNIZE POISONOUS PLANTS

NE OF THE BEST reasons to head out into the wild is to take in the breathtaking beauty Mother Nature has to offer. But while the lush landscapes of the wilderness may be a feast for your eyes, some of the flowers and plants composing the scenery can be harmful to your health. Follow these guidelines to learn when you should look but not touch.

1. *SAFETY IN NUMBERS*
Poison ivy and poison oak are among the most commonly encountered poisonous plants, but fortunately, some quick counting can often help you identify them. While not perfectly scientific, the old adage "Leaves of three, let it be!" can help you remember what to look for—though you should still proceed with caution as some species of both contain more than three leaves. Meanwhile, some plants such as poison sumac can have as many as 13 leaves but still give you an itchy rash upon contact. So generally, avoiding any plant with only three leaves is a good starting point for avoiding poisonous contact.

2. *UNSAFE SALAD*
While you can test a plant to see if it would be a suitable candidate to eat in a survival situation (pg. 62), sometimes it's better to play it safe. Avoid trying the food edibility test with any plants that produce a milky, white sap when

John Wayne and Paul Fix in the 1945 film *Back to Bataan*.

broken, as well as any that appear hairy, have shiny leaves or bear white berries. And as tempting as they may be, you should also steer clear of any mushrooms or berries you can't confidently identify.

3. *GOOD OL' GRASS*

If you need to give your legs a break and are just looking for a spot to sit or lay down in, a patch or field of grass is always a safe bet for avoiding poison. And, though it's not the most appetizing snack, you can also eat any kind of grass if you so choose. To get the most out of this meager meal, be sure to chew the leaves and swallow the juice they produce.

4. *SWEET RELIEF*

If you do come in contact with a poisonous plant and need a quick remedy for your itchy, rashy skin, look no further than the aftermath of your most recent campfire— charcoal can be quite useful in this situation (pg. 134).

HOW TO **HANDLE AN AVALANCHE**

HERE IS A rule in Special Forces that's important in any navigation but especially in winter: Plan your route. Do your homework to avoid areas with a known risk of avalanche. The best rule for all survival is prevention and avoidance. However, if you do find yourself in this dangerous situation, using these tools will maximize your chances of survival and rescue.

The following can be factors in a potential avalanche. Use them as warning signs before traversing a slope:

- An overhang of wet snow
- Recent cracks in the rock walls or ground
- The shady side of the mountain
- Steep terrain
- Recent rain
- A recent earthquake
- A recent avalanche
- Hollow-sounding snow
- Wind coming from behind a snowy overhang
- Backcountry and/or non-groomed terrain
- A foot or more of fresh snow on a steep face
- Local knowledge that the area is dangerous

IF YOU HAVE TO TRAVERSE through a risky area, you can do the following to better prepare yourself:

1. Pay attention to weather conditions: recent, current and forecast.

2. Travel with at least one other person.

3. Bring a cigarette lighter and a rope.

4. Traverse the slope as high up as you possibly can.

5. Connect yourself by rope to your teammate(s) and stay connected.

6. Plan a route that will take you as close as possible to large, solid objects like boulders and trees and stay uphill of them.

IF YOUR POWERS of prevention have failed you and you find yourself caught in an avalanche, here are the tools that will give you the best chance for survival:

1. Jump uphill of any crack that forms in your presence.

2. Get to the edge of the slope as soon as possible. The avalanche will funnel the snow down the center, creating a trough.

3. Kick off your skis, snowboard, snow shoes and let go of your poles and backpack.

4. Grab on to anything you pass, such as a tree or a boulder.

5. "Swim" perpendicular to the cascading snow in an effort to stay on top of it.

6. If you feel yourself getting buried, cover your face with your hands and try to create space for a pocket of air. Make your body as big as possible: Inhale to inflate your lungs. Spread your elbows apart. Nod your head back and forth in exaggerated movements to create as much space for wiggling as you can.

7. Light the lighter to determine which direction is up.

8. Begin to dig and, if possible, punch your hand up as far as it will go to create a ventilation shaft.

9. Do not fight or exhaust yourself. Conserve your strength until the avalanche has stopped and then use it to tunnel out.

HOW TO **HANDLE A VOLCANO**

 OHN WAYNE spent plenty of time in Hawaii and, fortunately, never had to deal with an erupting volcano during a visit. If you're traveling to one of the places in the world where this is a very real concern, you can maximize your safety by doing some research beforehand. Make a plan for evacuation and communications.

It's always a good idea to have a bug-out bag. You will need:
- A face mask or smoke hood
- Goggles that seal
- A long-sleeve shirt
- Long pants
- Medical supplies
- A flashlight
- A radio
- Water
- Food

1. Wear as much protective clothing as you can, such as long pants, long sleeves and a face mask.

2. Have a plan of evacuation that does not include motor vehicles or airplanes, since ash clogs engines and lava melts rubber tires.

3. Put distance and terrain between yourself and the lava flow. Be aware of its flow path.

4. Take the high road, if you can. Lava and water flow downhill. Be aware of irregular water levels and flow paths.

John Wayne, Gail Russell and Hawaiian surf legend Duke Kahanamoku (seated, right) in *Wake of the Red Witch* (1948). Hawaii is home to Mauna Loa, the largest active volcano on Earth.

5. If you are in a safe facility, keep all the windows and doors tightly sealed to keep out as much ash as possible.

6. Turn off the environmental system and close all vents.

7. Close the fireplace flue.

8. Listen to the radio for updates

9. Stay hydrated.

10. Tend to any open wounds (pg. 234) or burns immediately to prevent developing an infection (pg. 241).

11. Stay inside until there is an announcement that it's safe to venture outdoors.

12. If need be, seek medical attention.

13. Make sure you are cleared before heading back into the affected area.

14. Take care of your physical needs: eat, sleep, water, etc.

HOW TO **HANDLE A FOREST FIRE**

 OREST FIRES can happen anywhere and have dozens of known causes. Prevention is key. Green Beret woodcraft dictates that you clear a 10-foot swath around your intended fire. Keep an entrenching tool on hand and pay attention to the root system if you choose a below-ground method. If you do find yourself surrounded by a growing forest fire, there are still some things you can do for your own safety.

You will need:
- A heavy mylar blanket (to use as emergency shelter)
- A wet cloth

1. Cover your nose and mouth with wet cloth.

2. If you can, put a river, creek, stream, pond or lake between you and the fire.

3. Find an area of mud or dirt without anything growing in it. Wrap yourself in your emergency blanket/shelter and stay in the center of the dirt. Make sure not to touch any vegetation.

4. Find a ditch, ravine, gully or other low spot. Lie face down and cover your body with wet clothing, soil or mud.

5. Stay down until the fire passes.

John Wayne and Jim Hutton in *Hellfighters* (1968). The two actors also shared the screen in *The Green Berets* that year.

HOW TO **HANDLE MAMMALIAN PREDATORS**

 HILE PLAYING CARDS with Red Buttons on location for his African safari film *Hatari!* (1952), John Wayne was visited by a leopard. Unphased, Duke simply quipped to his co-star, "Buttons, see what he wants." Despite how things shook out for John Wayne, you want to avoid contact with wildlife. Keep the area around you clean and free from food smells by either destroying or removing food from your site (pg. 100). Hang all of your food and anything else you have that produces a scent in a bear bag at least 100 meters downwind from where you sleep. If possible, don't sleep in or with the same clothes you were wearing when you cooked your meal. Do not approach any kind of baby animal. Set your perimeter alarms (pgs. 166-169) and do not willingly feed any kind of wildlife.

If you do encounter an angry mammal, here are some things you can do.

1. Do not close the distance between yourself and the animal. Stand your ground or back away with slow deliberate movements. Keep your eye on the animal.

2. Do not turn your back or run away.

3. Leave the animal a way out. A cornered animal will fight more viciously.

4. Make noise. Be scary.

5. Make yourself as large as possible. Wave your arms or your jacket over your head. Stand on tiptoe.

6. Shed a piece of clothing and throw it far from you as a distraction. Some animals will move to inspect it closely because it smells like you. Use this as your window of opportunity to get away.

7. Stay on your feet. If you go down, they will have an absolute advantage.

8. Do not allow yourself to be surrounded.

9. Use trees and rocks to your advantage. Put them between you and the animal and/or climb them.

10. If you can, move upwind. This may seem counterintuitive, but humans are not normal prey and your scent will help them identify you.

11. Use your knife, gun, club, machete, bear spray, stick, axe or anything else you have on hand to defend yourself. Aim for the animal's most tender parts: eyes, ears, nose and genitals.

John Wayne and a feline co-star on the set of *Hatari!* (1962).

HOW TO DEAL WITH A RABID ANIMAL

 NE OF THE MOST appealing aspects of heading out into the wild is the chance to escape mundane, predictable, everyday life. On the flip side of that, however, is the risk of encountering dangerous situations you might not deal with every day. While most people are familiar with the virus known as rabies, they most likely haven't encountered a rabid animal unless they're a veterinarian or someone who works in animal control. If you haven't been in such a situation yourself, these guidelines can help you learn what to look for and what to do.

1. Rabies only occurs in mammals, which means you don't have to worry about contracting rabies when dealing with wild birds, reptiles, amphibians and fish. You should, however, be mindful of this threat whenever you encounter the likes of wild dogs, raccoons, foxes, coyotes, bats and skunks.

2. One of the first ways you can spot rabies in an animal is by observing their demeanor when they see you. If a wild animal seems unafraid as you enter its territory, do not continue to approach it. Even if the animal doesn't exhibit other tell-tale signs of rabies, this unusually calm behavior could indicate a rabies infection.

3. Some animals will show more obvious signs of rabies than others. In California, for example, rabies virus is most frequently found in skunks and bats. If you see one of these

nocturnal creatures out being active during the day, that's likely a good indication that they are rabid. Unusually calm behavior could also indicate a rabies infection.

4. Saliva is the transmitter between rabid animals and humans. Even if the animal doesn't bite you, you can still contract rabies if the saliva gets in an open cut or your eyes, nose or mouth.

5. If you are bitten or scratched by an animal that seems to be rabid, immediately wash the wound with soap and water. Try to remember as many details as possible about the animal and be prepared to evacuate in order to receive medical attention.

HOW TO **HANDLE REPTILIAN PREDATORS**

 EPTILES HUNT and attack very differently than their mammalian counterparts. Never purposely enter a reptile's territory. Avoid the watering holes, feeding grounds, mating territory and dens of alligators, crocodiles, snakes and lizards.

ALLIGATORS AND CROCODILES

Alligators and crocodiles have wonderful night vision, are excellent swimmers, can move silently and can remain underwater for extremely long durations. If you are facing an alligator or a crocodile, these are some additional things you need to know.

1. Most of their muscles are designed to close their mouths and very few are dedicated to opening them. If you can grab hold of their closed mouth and clamp it closed, you have the advantage. If you have duct tape, even better. You can wrap a few layers of duct tape around their closed mouth and they are at your mercy.

2. Alligators and crocodiles rely on peripheral vision and there is a place directly in front of their nose where they can't see at all. If you need to stand still, stand there.

3. Their claws are sharp but their legs are short and they are not flexible creatures. If you tape their snout shut, they can't reach you with their claws.

4. Likewise, due to their inflexibility, they can't reach their tail with their mouth. If you grab hold of the end of an alligator's tail, they will thrash around but they cannot get to you. They are stronger than you are though, so hold on for dear life.

5. Alligators and crocodiles are also fast. Never challenge one to catch you. They will.

6. Alligators stick together. Where there's one, there's two.

SNAKES

1. Do not question whether or not it's a threat. If you see a snake and can kill it from a distance, that is your best option. A shotgun works better than a rifle or a handgun because snakes don't make a very large target and are often on the move. If you don't have a projectile weapon, use a reaching weapon such as a machete.

2. It is highly unusual for a human to be hunted by a snake. Snakes attack when they are threatened or attacked. Unfortunately, sometimes you find them by accidentally stepping on them, which causes them to attack. Be vigilant. Know what kinds of snakes are around and where they sleep. Avoid those places. If you are attacked by a great snake like an anaconda, a boa constrictor or a python, you will need to gain control of the head. Severing it would be best. If you can't do that without harming yourself as well, strike the eyes and grab the back of its head. Lock your elbow out to keep the head an arm's length away from you and lead the rest of the body to uncoil by directing the head. Where the head goes, the body will follow.

3. Remember that a severed snake's head can still produce and inject venom. Do not handle the severed head of a poisonous snake.

HOW TO
RECOGNIZE
VENOMOUS
SNAKES

 CCORDING TO estimates by the Centers for Disease Control and Prevention, between 7,000 and 8,000 people in the U.S. get bitten by venomous snakes each year. To make sure you don't end up contributing to this statistic, here's what you need to know.

In most cases, venomous snakes won't go out of their way to bite you—but they might if you accidentally step on them. As you watch for poisonous plants on your path (pg. 196), do your best to keep an eye out for any slithering reptiles that may be lurking. This is particularly tricky considering snakes are camouflage experts that react to hearing movement by staying still. But, once you know what you're looking for, you'll be better prepared for a potential encounter.

1. Research is key. While there are about 20 species of venomous snakes in North America, you'll want to focus on being able to recognize the ones found in your region before heading out. If you're walking around the Sonoran Desert of Arizona, you might see the vibrant western coral snake. In the northeast and sometimes beyond, you should be looking out for the copperhead, which ranges as far north as New York and as far west as Nebraska.

2. If you're able to in the moment, observe the snake's

markings and shape. Venomous snakes often have triangular heads, which they flatten when feeling threatened. If the snake's tail is more visible than its head, look for a rattle, as every type of rattlesnake is venomous. Some rattlesnakes lose their rattlers through age or injury, however, so continue with caution even if you don't see or hear a rattler. A snake's coloring—particularly its stripes—can also be useful to note, and you can remember this rhyme for when you need to differentiate between the coral snake and its harmless look-alike, the scarlet kingsnake: "Red to yellow, kill a fellow; red to black, venom lack."

3. Don't let your guard down while in the water—there are a few types of venomous snakes that swim, such as the yellow-bellied sea snake and the water moccasin, which is also called the cottonmouth. But rather than worrying about what lurks deep in the water, stay focused on the surface. If you see a snake swimming on the top of the water, simply get out of its way.

4. When in doubt, your best bet is to assume every snake you see slithering has the potential to take you out with a venomous bite. There's no sense in pushing your luck, pilgrim. Just steer clear.

John Wayne fends off reptile predators in a snake pit in *True Grit* (1969).

HOW TO **HANDLE AQUATIC PREDATORS**

 HARKS AND WHALES are like other species in that they have types of prey upon which they usually feed. Humans are not on the list. However, if you show up in their hunting ground at feeding time, you are at risk. Know what kinds of sharks and whales are in the local waters, what they eat and what time they hunt. As terrifying as these creatures can be, they do have vulnerabilities.

SHARKS

1. Sharks have very sensitive snouts, eyelids and gills. If you need to attack, aim for those.

2. Sharks close their eyes when they open their mouths to take a bite. You can use that timing to your advantage. In an ideal situation, you would try to strike the shark in any of its sensitive areas the instant it closes its eyes, before it opens its mouth.

3. While it is true that sharks are attracted to blood, what really gets them is any kind of noise, commotion or movement, such as the vibrations made by dying fish. Be still and avoid making any such vibrations.

4. Sharks feed on what is above them, not at their level or below. If you can descend, you can get out of the danger zone.

John Wayne battles
a giant squid in *Reap
the Wild Wind* (1942).
Proceeds from the
film's premiere were
donated to the Navy
Relief Fund.

HOW TO HANDLE AQUATIC PREDATORS *continued*

WHALES

1. Whale attacks are less common, but they do happen. Orcas have been known to attack boats near them in the water. Your best chance of surviving a whale attack is to get out of the water. Whales travel in pods—if you see one, more are likely to be nearby.

2. A whale's eyes are as sensitive as anyone else's.

3. Whales are stiff and inflexible, so getting to the dorsal fin side is an advantage.

PIRANHAS

1. Despite what some movies may want you to believe, piranha attacks are quite unlikely, but that doesn't mean you should take this sharp-toothed water predator lightly if you happen to be exploring the waters of South America. Piranhas have strong jaws and razor-sharp, triangular teeth quite similar to a shark's, so you obviously don't want to find yourself on the receiving end of their bite.

2. The two species of piranha considered the most dangerous are the red-bellied piranha, because it is the most abundant and travels in a large group, and the black piranha, which has the most powerful bite of all species of this fierce fish.

3. Avoid getting in waters with piranha populations if you have a cut or an open wound. Like sharks, piranhas are drawn to blood. And if you're swimming, try not to thrash around in the water too much as piranhas might attribute this type of movement to their typical prey, which includes various fish, crustaceans and insects.

4. If a piranha does bite you, it will usually be a single bite rather than a continuous attack. When this occurs, get out of the water as quickly as possible—that one bite is likely to draw quite a bit of blood, which will attract other piranhas in the area. Once you're out of the water, treat the wound (pg. 240).

JELLYFISH

1. According to statistics, jellyfish sting approximately 150 million people around the world each year. While their stings are often treatable and rarely life-threatening, they are painful and best to be avoided. If you packed a wetsuit or other protective swimwear that covers the body, wear it in waters that may contain jellyfish.

2. If you spot a jellyfish, quickly swim in the opposite direction. Be mindful of your outstretched limbs, though, as even the slightest brush against one of this creature's tentacles can cause the jellyfish to release venom from its thousands of microscopic barbed stingers.

3. If you experience the following symptoms after being in the ocean, you could be experiencing the effects of jellyfish sting: burning/itching/stinging sensation, swelling, tracks on the skin that are red, purple or brown in color. More severe symptoms may include: nausea, difficulty breathing, feeling faint or drowsy, muscle pain or spasms, heart irregularities.

4. Most jellyfish stings can be treated by carefully plucking the stinger and soaking the skin in purified hot water (pg. 34). Do not rinse with urine or seawater, and do not apply alcohol or pressure bandages to the affected area. In any case, it's best to seek medical attention as soon as possible.

TIPS FOR WATER CROSSING AND WATER-PROOFING

FORDING A RIVER or a stream can be challenging and dangerous if you don't know what to do. Never enter rushing water and never swim a river unless you have to. Keep in mind that water can be deeper in some spots and shallower in others. Proceed with caution for every step you take. Look as far downstream as you can and check for anything you might get swept into.

To waterproof your pack and cross a river, you will need:
- 2 large plastic bags or ponchos and lashing
- A sturdy stick about the length of your leg
- A rope wider than the river crossing (optional)

1. Look for a straight, wide, shallow section of river to cross. Water speeds up in narrow places.

2. Waterproof your pack with two plastic bags or ponchos, which will turn your pack into a flotation device. A best practice is to line your backpack with a plastic garbage bag just as you would line a trash can. Place all your gear into the plastic liner, blow some air into it and tie it closed. Then close your backpack.

TIPS FOR WATER CROSSING AND WATER-PROOFING   *continued*

3. Twist the hood opening into a gooseneck and double the neck back on itself, tying it closed with a lashing. Lay the poncho out flat and place your pack in the center. Fold the poncho in half by joining the edges together around the pack. Fold the joined edges over by 2 inches then fold them over and over until they are tight against the pack. Close each end with a waterproof gooseneck and tie the ends to each other with tension. Put the whole pack down onto a second poncho, seam down, and repeat the whole process with this second layer.

4. Float your pack in front of you and steer it. Make sure you can let go easily if it becomes a liability. Green Berets keep their packs water-proofed at all times.

5. To reduce drag in the water, you can take items of clothing off and store them in your water-proofed pack.

6. Use a stout stick as your third leg—a tripod is very hard to knock over. Hold the stick in front of you and use it to check the depth before you take each step.

7. If you have three people and a rope wider than the river crossing, you can cross as a team by tying the rope around the strongest person. The remaining two should keep hold of the rope and keep the slack out of it, letting it out one foot at a time as the strong person crosses. If anything happens, immediately pull them back to shore. Once the first person has crossed, the second person can use the line to cross, pulling themselves hand over hand. The last person should tie the rope around their chest and the first two can pull them across.

n Wayne in *Rooster
burn* (1975). The
 was shot in Bend,
gon, Deschutes
ional Forest, the
cade Mountains
 the Rogue River.

HOW TO ESCAPE A RIPTIDE

OHN WAYNE had a love for the Pacific Ocean as deep as its waters, but he also respected the deadly dangers that lurk in the vast body of water. While many people may assume predators such as sharks are the greatest danger when swimming in the sea, the greatest threat swimmers face in the ocean is actually silent and invisible: riptides.

Each year, more than 100 Americans are killed by riptides, incredibly strong currents that can pull even the strongest swimmers far out to sea. Escaping one can be not just physically challenging, but also mentally challenging as it involves going against some of your body's natural reactions to harm. But if you follow these guidelines, you can increase your chances of survival.

1. As soon as you realize you're caught in a riptide, do your best not to fight against it. Though this indeed goes against all of our natural survival instincts, it is crucial— fighting a riptide will quickly exhaust you while doing little to actually help you escape. These deadly currents pull at a rate of 8 feet per second, which eliminates the option of swimming to safety. Try to stay calm by keeping in mind that a riptide can't pull you underwater, only farther out to sea.

2. Rather than frantically trying to swim toward the shore, calmly but purposefully swim parallel to the shore instead. While seemingly counterproductive, this is key to your escape. Although currents are very strong, they're also very narrow, which leaves you room to get away. And even

Elizabeth Allen and John Wayne in *Donovan's Reef* (1963), the last film Duke made with his longtime mentor, director John Ford.

if the current does pull you a little farther out, don't panic. Once you've escaped the riptide, you can still get back to shore if you've conserved your energy by not fighting against the current.

3. As you make your way back to dry land, swim diagonally to the shore at an angle away from the current to ensure that you don't become caught in the current again.

HOW TO STOP A SLIDE DOWN AN ICY INCLINE

HERE IS ONE tried and true technique for arresting a descent down an icy slope (apart from losing your footing and sliding headlong into a crevasse). It's called a glissade, and every ice climber knows it by heart. If you're heading someplace slippery, you should know it too, pilgrim.

1. Sit down on your backside, lean back and bend your knees slightly. This will give you the most control and the ability to see and attempt to steer.

2. Dig your heels in below you and your ice axe above you to gain some control over your speed.

3. If you are struggling to stop your descent, aim your feet for a tree or a rock that can help you stop, but make sure to absorb the shock by bending your knees so you don't risk breaking your back.

4. A glissade can cause an avalanche, so if the snow seems to be moving with you, pitch yourself to the side and roll as far away from its path as you can. Remember, since avalanches funnel the center, you'll want to aim for the edge.

5. If your feet don't stop your slide, hug your ice axe close to your body with the pick over your shoulder, roll over and dig in as hard as you can.

John Wayne in *Island in the Sky* (1953). Decca Records released a 10-inch disc featuring music by Emil Newman and narrations by John Wayne to promote the film.

TIPS FOR
TRAVERSING
SNOW AND ICE

ACH SEASON has its share of dangers, but winter hazards are the most treacherous. Plan for warmth, hydration, appropriate caloric intake for the temperature and medical care before heading out.

1. Beware of holes and tree wells in fresh snow. They can cave in and swallow you.

2. Use ski poles, walking/hiking sticks or two good sized sticks to give you more stability and reduce your workload.

3. Avoid any cliffs or other shear faces from above or below.

4. Do not walk out onto ice that is less than 4 inches thick.

5. If hiking in mountains or hills, stay uphill of trees and boulders. Move uphill of any crack that forms. Carry an ice pick.

6. Try to travel at night or first thing in the morning when you can walk on top of the icy crust. If you must travel in the middle of the day, try to walk in the shade.

7. Wear "Yak tracks"—slipover traction cleats—on your hiking books to add grip and stability.

John Wayne in
The Big Trail (1930).
The film was inspired
by a *Saturday Evening
Post* serial by Hal G.
Evarts called "The
Shaggy Legion."

HOW TO SURVIVE FALLING INTO ICY WATER

 NE OF THE defining characteristics of a silver screen John Wayne character is their ability to stay calm and confident in a dire situation. If you can muster that same strength should you fall through thin ice into the freezing water below, you can give yourself a fighting chance.

1. The moment your body hits the freezing water, you're going to enter what's known as "cold shock." These physiological changes will include an adrenaline surge and skyrocketing heart rate, which can cause you to have a hyperventilation reflex. To put up your best fight against these reflexes, get your head above water as quickly as possible. It only takes about 1 to 3 minutes before your body begins to have severe reactions to the dangerous temperature it finds itself in.

2. At this point, your body is in an intense battle against the cold's debilitating effects on muscle coordination and movement. The hole you fell through will be your best chance to exit the water, so focus on finding it and then swim to it as fast as you can once you do. As you swim upward and out of the hole, put as much of your upper body on the surface of the ice as possible, then repeatedly kick your legs as you simultaneously pull yourself up out of the water with your arms.

3. While it will be a huge relief to make it out of the water, avoid celebrating just yet. You've already fallen through that ice once, which means it can happen again. Roll away from the opening and get yourself onto sturdy ground. You now have to address your dropping core body temperature, which can still kill you even though you've reached dry land. Seek warm, dry shelter—and if you haven't built shelter yet, even a tree will do for now.

4. As long as you're wearing your soaked clothes, hypothermia can still claim your life. To ensure you're receiving as much warmth as possible from your heat sources, strip everything off. To conserve your body heat, cross your arms across your chest and tuck your knees up to your chest. As your wet clothes dry, change into dry clothes if you have them and build yourself a fire (pgs. 102-137) for more warmth.

John Wayne and Marsha Hunt in *Born to the West* (1937). The film is based on a novel of the same name by Zane Grey.

FIRST
AID

**THESE TIPS CAN HELP
YOU HANDLE INJURIES
AND ILLNESSES IN A
HEARTBEAT.**

HOW TO **MAKE A TOURNIQUET**

PECIAL FORCES medics use the principle of "high and tight" when placing a tourniquet for multiple reasons. If a tourniquet is placed as high up on the limb as it can go, it will cover any bleed below it, reducing the time by valuable, life-saving seconds. Still, it should only be resorted to if absolutely necessary.

You will need:
- A piece of material (bandana, T-shirt, pants, belt, towel, thin blanket, pillowcase—many options will work)
- A stick about 6 inches long

1. Wrap your material as high as possible on the arm or leg. Start in the middle of the tourniquet material and wrap both ends around the limb in opposite directions.

2. Tie half an overhand knot and place your stick right over the knot. Tie the other half of the knot, tying the stick to the material.

3. Use the stick as a windlass and turn it to tighten it down until the bleeding stops and there is no pulse in that limb.

4. Use the tails of the material to tie the stick in place by wrapping one tail around one end of the stick clockwise and the other tail around the other end of the stick counterclockwise. Tie the last of the tail into a knot.

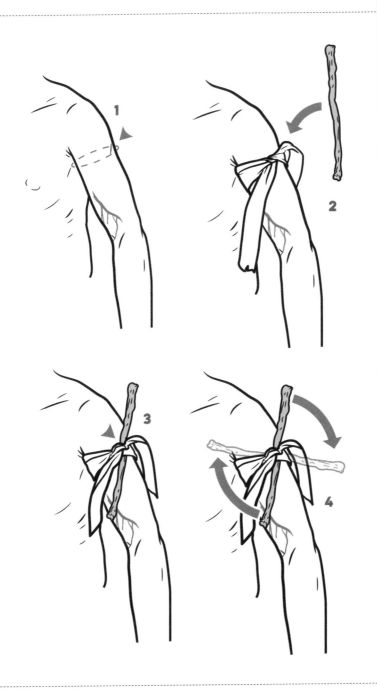

HOW TO **PACK A WOUND AND MAKE PRESSURE DRESSING**

 ACKING A WOUND is not an enviable job, but it can be necessary to save a life. The person may holler or even faint, but what you do may keep them alive.

You will need:
- 3 long strips of clean cloth material

1. Tie a small knot into the end of one piece of material. With your finger, reach deeply into the wound to find the source of the bleeding. Take the knot of the material and stuff it into the wound, directly onto the blood source. Begin to feed the entire strip of material into the wound as tightly as possible. It needs to fill the entire hole. A good rule to follow is to pack north, south, east, west and repeat. This ensures you have packed tightly against all the walls of tissue in the open wound.

2. If you have any of the packing material left over when the wound is completely filled, bunch it up and press it firmly on the surface of the wound. Take the second strip of material and bunch it up, combine it with the material already there and place it directly over the wound. Hold it firmly in place, or have the patient hold it.

3. Take the last strip of material and wrap it tightly around

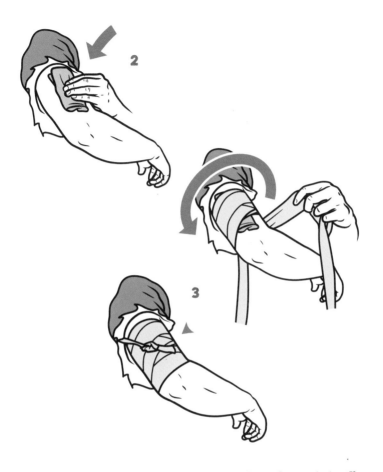

the limb or body, holding all your work in place. Tie it off with the knot directly over the wound.

NOTE Packing a wound can only be done on certain parts of the body like the fleshy parts of the arms and legs, shoulders and hips (front and back). Never pack a head, chest or abdominal wound. You may be out there all alone and therefore have to do all of this for yourself. Carry those strips of cloth material or be willing to sacrifice an article of clothing to save your life. Be prepared, pilgrim.

HOW TO **CLOSE** A WOUND

 HE PURPOSE of closing a wound is to connect two pieces of tissue that should be one so that they can heal. It's also crucial to keep the wound closed because dirt and debris carry bacteria that can cause infection, and developing an infection in the wilderness can be a life-threatening problem.

You will need:
- Duct tape
- Zip ties

1. Never close a dirty wound. Flush the wound with copious amounts of clean water to ensure there is no bacteria, dirt or debris in it.

2. Do not close a wound in the field unless it's a last resort. Whenever possible, leave it for professional medical staff to do in a controlled environment with a sterile field.

3. The most expedient wound-closer in the field is not invasive and can be premade and carried along with you. Take two strips of duct tape and place them on each side of the wound, as close as possible to the open edges.

4. Tear off two more duct tape strips and lay them down, sticky side up. Cut the female ends off a few zip ties and place them at intervals along the edge of one sticky side (4A). Put the corresponding bodies of the zip ties at the same intervals along the other strip's sticky side (4B). The broad end should be well-seated on the tape and the narrow end should be sticking out by a lot.

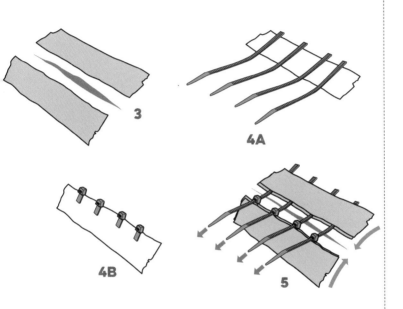

5. Place the tape and zip tie combination down directly on the first layer of tape, one one each side. The sticky side should be down, capturing the zip tie pieces between the two pieces of tape. Place each male end across the wound and into the corresponding female end. After they are all aligned, pull them closed.

NOTE These days, you can prepare for potential wounds by purchasing ready-to-use wound-closers such as butterfly strips, steri-strips and zip-stitches. Skin glue and super glue also work well.

HOW TO
MAKE A SPLINT

HERE ARE NUMEROUS ways to make a splint in the wilderness. You always want to splint the joints above and below the injured area, so choose sticks that will meet that need. In some cases, the sticks may need to be two different lengths. Limbs are tapered, so you must take care to tie your splint snugly enough that it will not slip off but not so tight as to impede circulation. Never tie your knots directly over the injury or on a joint, but above and below it.

You will need:
- Straight sticks of varying widths and lengths
- Long strips of clean material

1. For a wrist or forearm injury, you will want to immobilize the hand, wrist, forearm and elbow if you can. You may need to get creative as no one wants their elbow to be immobilized while straightened. You can do this by choosing two sticks that go from the patient's palm to past their elbow. Place one on the palm side of the arm and the other on the back-of-the-hand side. Tie one knot below the wrist around the hand, holding the sticks in place. Tie another above the wrist or above the place of the suspected break. Use a length of material to tie a sling so the patient can take the weight off their injured arm and carry it with their neck instead. Check the fingernails for good capillary return: Upon pinching the fingernail and letting it go, color should return in no more than three seconds.

2. If the injury is to the upper arm (humerus), splint the humerus to the shoulder in front and in back. Tie your

knots above the elbow and at the armpit and make a sling wide enough for the patient's entire forearm. Taking the weight off will go a long way toward reducing their pain. Unless you have stiff material at a right angle, you won't be able to splint past the elbow, but putting the forearm in the sling will help. You can finish the immobilization by tying a swath around the sling. This will go on the outside of the injured humerus, around the patient, and tie off around their ribs opposite the injured side. Be gentle as you are tying a swath right around the injury. Leave the uninjured arm free.

3. For a foot or ankle injury, leave the boot (or other sturdy footwear) on. Footwear that goes above the ankle will help create support, and you won't be able to get it back on if you take it off. Use two sticks that reach from the bottom of the foot up past the knee. Place them on the inside and outside of the leg. Take the middle of one of the cloth strips and place it under the ball of the injured foot. Bring the ends around the top on the left and right. Cross them into an X pattern on top of the foot and tie them off behind the ankle. Tie the sticks just above the ankle, mid calf, just below and just above the knee.

4. For a knee injury, run the sticks from ankle to groin on the inside and ankle to hip on the outside. Tie your strips at the ankle, mid calf, just below and above the knee and up at the top of the femur.

5. For a hip injury, run the sticks from the ankle or the mid calf to the groin on one side and ankle to the top of the ribcage on the outside. Tie the strips at the ankle, mid calf, above and below the knee, at the top of the femur, around the abdomen and around the chest. Be very careful not to tie the top ones too tight and never impede anyone's breathing.

6. Finger splints are tiny versions of the same thing. You can use one very little stick and small strips of cloth or even duct tape.

HOW TO
DEAL WITH
DISLOCATIONS

VEN THE ROUGHEST and toughest among us would agree a dislocated bone doesn't feel all that great. Always address a dislocation as soon as it occurs—if you allow any time to pass, the surrounding muscles will clamp down, making reduction difficult (and in some cases impossible) later on. The more rapid your response, the better your results. The key to all of these is to move gently, slowly and steadily once your hands are on the patient.

You will need:
- A 5-pound rock
- A 10-pound rock
- Long strips of clean material

1. For a finger or toe, ask the person to flex the injured digit. Take the very tip of the affected digit and pull out slowly and consistently until the bone clears the socket. You don't need to clear it by much. Keeping that same consistent traction, gently lower the finger or toe back into the socket.

2. For a knee, have the person lay back and brace their good leg on something solid. Take the foot of the injured leg in both hands and use the same technique. Apply slow and steady traction until the patella pops back into place and then let the traction off just as slowly and steadily.

3. For a shoulder, you can start with the same technique. Lay the person on their back and take their hand in both of

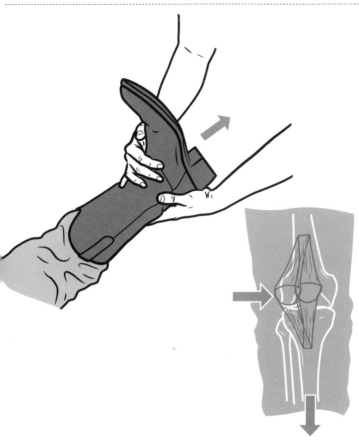

yours. Standing over them, apply that same old slow and steady traction out and back in. If the shoulder will not comply, you can find a place for the patient to lay down on their stomach with the affected arm hanging down free. Choose a rock weighing about 5 pounds and tie it to their wrist, slowly and gently transferring the weight from your hand to their arm. Allow it to hang freely for about 20 minutes while they attempt to relax their muscles. If the muscles can relax, the rock will successfully reduce the dislocation. If that doesn't work, you can move to a bigger rock. Only do that once. If the heavier rock fails to fix it, you will need to seek medical care.

HOW TO **TREAT BITES AND STINGS**

OMETIMES THE smallest things in nature can make a big impact. Whether it's a bite from a spider, ant or centipede or a sting from a bee or a wasp, the field treatment will be the same.

You will need:
- Antihistamine
- Pain reliever
- Anti-itch cream
- Soap and clean water

1. For all insect and spider bites and stings, start by taking an antihistamine.

2. Clean the affected area with soap and lots of clean water.

3. Remove the stinger. If you have an alcoholic beverage handy, pour it over the affected area to help kill bacteria.

4. Take pain medicine and apply anti-itch cream as needed.

5. Watch for signs of an allergic reaction like stomach cramping, hives or respiratory distress. Seek medical help if needed.

6. If the offending insect or spider was poisonous, you will need immediate medical care complete with anti-venom or anti-neural toxins before the wound becomes life-threatening.

HOW TO TREAT INFECTIONS AND RASHES

NFECTIONS COME from the bacteria in anything and everything around you. Rashes can be allergic or non-allergic. In the wilderness, it's difficult to treat infections and rashes comprehensively. But if you come prepared, you can buy yourself some time before seeking medical attention.

You will need:
- Antihistamine
- Soap and clean water
- Topical antibiotic
- Clean bandages

1. If you develop a rash or a suspected infection in the field, take an antihistamine and start watching for signs of an allergic reaction.

2. Clean the area with soap and water. You can also use drinking alcohol if soap and water aren't available.

3. Apply topical antibiotic to the suspected infection and bandage it loosely to keep it protected from dirt and debris.

4. Be prepared to seek medical attention.

HOW TO **TREAT CLIMATE-BASED INJURIES**

EATHER-RELATED injuries are serious and can be life-threatening. There are multiple possible injuries that can occur in both cold and hot climates. As soon as you identify symptoms, cease your activity and begin countermeasures. It might save your life.

HOT CLIMATE INJURIES

1. Heat cramps are usually the first indicator that a person is headed toward a heat injury. However, this is not always the case. Heat cramps come on painfully in conditions where physical work is being done in hot environments. The loss of electrolytes through sweat is the trigger. Although these involuntary muscle spasms can occur in any muscle group, they are most often felt in the calves, arms, abdomen and back. If you experience any of these, stop the physical labor, find a cool place to sit down and rest, rehydrate with electrolytes and gently stretch the affected muscles. Do not resume the physical activity for several hours. Although heat cramps are not dangerous themselves, they are a painful warning that you're headed toward heat exhaustion and losing electrolytes faster than you are replacing them.

2. Heat exhaustion begins with dehydration and is characterized by overheating. The symptoms include rapid heart rate, profuse sweating, red (flushed) skin,

Harry Carey, Jr. and John Wayne in the 1948 John Ford film *3 Godfathers*. Filmed in one of the hottest places on Earth, the punishing desert valley region of Death Valley, California, the film sees Duke as Robert Hightower, an outlaw on the run with his partners after robbing a bank. In the desert, the troublesome trio encounter a dying mother and her baby, whom they vow to bring to safety. But after the harsh climate takes the lives of his partners, Hightower is alone in his battle against dehydration as he fights to make it to town with the infant in tow.

HOW TO TREAT CLIMATE-BASED INJURIES *continued*

panting, cool and moist skin, goosebumps, dizziness, faintness, fatigue, a weak pulse, muscle cramps, nausea and headache. The treatment is simple and straightforward: Stop all activity, rest, move to a cooler place and rehydrate.

3. Heat stroke is the most serious of the heat injuries. It occurs when a person is seriously overheated (104 degrees Fahrenheit or 40 degrees Celsius) and can lead to paralysis and death. The signs and symptoms of heatstroke are high body temperature, altered mental state, absence of sweat, nausea and vomiting, flushed skin, panting, elevated heart rate and headache. A heat stroke can be brought on by a high ambient temperature or by excessive physical exertion. It is exacerbated by dehydration. If it is caused by ambient temperature, the skin will be hot and dry. If it is brought on by physical exertion, the skin may feel tacky. In all cases, heat stroke is a life threatening injury and needs emergency medical care. Untreated, it can damage the kidneys, heart, brain and muscles. If you have these signs or symptoms, immediately stop all work, get to the coldest possible place, remove all excess clothing, get the body temperature down by any means necessary: ice, water, fan, shade, etc. Place ice or cold, wet towels under the armpits, on the groin, on the head and on the back of the neck. Place a barrier between the ice and the skin to prevent frostbite. Do not immerse in ice water as this can cause shock. Evacuate to a hospital.

COLD CLIMATE INJURIES

1. A common misconception about hypothermia is that it can only occur in seriously cold weather. When you consider that the average body temperature needs to remain at 98.6 degrees Fahrenheit, you can see how hypothermia can actually occur in temperatures that feel comfortable.

Hypothermia is simply a condition in which the body loses heat faster than it can replace it. A person is technically hypothermic when their body temperature reaches 95 degrees Fahrenheit. Hypothermia is an emergency and requires immediate intervention and medical care. Signs of hypothermia include shivering; slurred speech; slow, shallow breathing; weak pulse; clumsiness/lack of coordination; drowsiness; low energy; confusion; loss of consciousness; bright red and cold skin (in babies); and a feeling of inner warmth. If you encounter these symptoms, get to a warmer place. Move gently, as jarring movements can trigger irregular heartbeats. Remove wet clothing and wrap up in warm and dry blankets.

Try to be aware of confused or risky behavior. A person suffering from hypothermia is usually disoriented and will not be able to make productive decisions. In fact, since they are already feeling warm, they may begin to remove clothing and/or try to immerse themselves in cold water. Be prepared. If you are in a wilderness setting, keep moving. The warm, drowsy feeling you're experiencing will cause you to want to lay down and sleep. Do not do so. Build a fire and get close to it. It's better to go naked than to stay in wet clothes. Your priorities are heat, dry clothing or blankets and preventing impaired decisions.

2. Frostbite is a very serious condition that can often result in the loss of body parts. It is a literal freezing of the skin and underlying tissue. Frostbite is most common in fingers, toes, nose, ears, cheeks and chins, but it can occur anywhere. The signs of frostbite include initially cold skin with a prickly sensation progressing to numbness, red, white, blue, grey, or yellow skin, hard and waxy looking skin, clumsiness due to muscle stiffness and blistering after rewarming. If you encounter frostbite, move to a warmer place and add layers of thermal clothing. Never rub the skin as it can damage the tissue. Place the affected area in between your legs or under your arms. Bring the temperature of the affected area up slowly with lukewarm water and evacuate to medical care.

HOW TO **REMEDY** INGESTED POISON

 EVER UNDERESTIMATE Mother Nature, pilgrim: Plants, animals and even insects can be poisonous. If you suspect you've ingested something poisonous in the field, there are a couple things you can do.

You will need:
- Charcoal
- Water

1. Some poisons are best evacuated from the body by the most expeditious route, and some are better left inside and absorbed by an added substance. If you have time in advance, do some research to figure out which poisons are in the area and how each should be handled.

2. If you need to evacuate a poison rapidly, induce vomiting. It will take your hydration down but it will rid your body of the harmful substance. It's a good idea to carry ipecac or hydrogen peroxide to induce vomiting in the field.

3. If the poison is better left in place and absorbed, you can make a charcoal cocktail and drink it. Take charcoal briquettes from your fire and crush them into powder, Mix them in water and drink it. The charcoal will bind to the poison and absorb it. Make sure to drink copious amounts of liquid. Charcoal is hard to pass and requires overhydration to do it successfully.

HOW TO INDUCE VOMITING

 HILE IT'S GOOD to be as prepared as possible before heading out into nature, odds are you won't be packing everything you could ever need. Ipecac or hydrogen peroxide are ideal for situations in which you need to induce vomiting, but you should know some alternative methods in case you don't have those substances on hand.

1. A combination of physics and psychology can be useful when you need to vomit. If you spin in circles rapidly, you can give yourself motion sickness, which can cause vomiting. To expedite this unpleasant process, try graphically envisioning yourself or someone else vomiting.

2. You can also make yourself vomit without the aid of any substances by simply enacting your gag reflex. Lean forward and gently reach into your mouth with one or two fingers, going as far back as you can. Move your fingers around to tickle the back of your throat. You will soon start to gag, and hopefully, vomit.

3. Do not induce vomiting if you have a condition that can cause seizures. Additionally, if the ingested substance is a corrosive acid or base, vomiting may not be the best option as it can damage your esophagus coming back up. In this case, defer to the charcoal method (opposite page) or evacuate and seek medical attention.

HOW TO
DEAL WITH
IMPALEMENTS

I F A FOREIGN object becomes lodged anywhere in your body, your instinct will likely be to remove it immediately—but that might not be the best idea. The situation will dictate the solution: If the object is large, removing it may cause life-threatening bleeding and/or irreparable damage to the surrounding tissue.

You will need:
  • Long strips of clean, strong material

1. If the impaled object is a fish hook in skin, you can cut the barb off and withdraw it the same way it went in. Clean the wound and treat the site for infection (pg. 241).

2. If the impaled object is in the eye, do not remove it. Evacuate to seek medical attention while doing your best to avoid touching or manipulating the impaled object along the way.

3. If the impaled object is deep in the flesh, leave it there and build padding around it with wadded up strips of cloth. Tie or tape the wadding down around the object but do not move it. The more it moves, the more it damages the surrounding tissue. Splint it in place (pg. 236) and evacuate to medical care.

4. If the impaled object has pinned you to something, cut it off as close as is reasonable to your flesh using slow movements to minimize harmful vibrations, and then splint it.

HOW TO **DEAL WITH TRAUMATIC AMPUTATION**

 RAUMATIC AMPUTATION in the field can be the result of something being torn off, cut off or bitten off. It may not produce much bleeding, but it is likely to induce shock.

You will need:
- Long strips of clean material
- Water

1. If a tourniquet is required, apply one right away (pg. 230).

2. Locate the missing part. Wrap it in clean, wet cloth.

3. Wrap the stump in clean cloth. Put the severed part somewhere it can be carried safely and covertly, as the sight of a severed limb increases the risk of shock.

4. Watch for shock and treat by resting and regulating the body temperature up or down as needed. Think and speak words of hope, calm and peace.

5. Evacuate to medical care.

6. If the abdomen is eviscerated, do not attempt to put anything back inside the body. Cover the abdomen loosely with a clean, wet cloth and evacuate.

7. If the missing body part is a tooth, the best place to keep it is back in the socket where it originated. If that is not possible, keep it wet in the owner's saliva until they can be seen by a dentist. If there is tissue attached to it, leave it all intact.

HOW TO **FLUSH YOUR EYE**

VEN THE TOUGHEST among us can admit that getting a foreign object or substance in the eye is quite unpleasant. Eyes are extremely sensitive, and even though you might be rushing to remove something irritating, you'll need to do so calmly and cautiously so as to not make matters worse. You don't want to end up looking like you're cosplaying as Rooster Cogburn year-round—save that for Halloween, pilgrim.

1. Fight the urge to rub your eye. This could cause the object to be pushed further into the eye, and it can also cause the object to scratch the cornea, resulting in even more prolonged pain.

2. Before making any attempts to remove the irritating object or substance from your eye, wash your hands. If you wear contact lenses, remove them as they may be aiding the culprit in sticking to the eye.

3. Gather some clean, warm water (pg. 34) and tilt your head to one side, not backward. Slowly pour the water into your eye or eyes and try to keep your eyes open as much as possible. Then tilt your head to the opposite side and repeat the process.

4. If you have a large enough bowl (pg. 32) or water-holding vessel, fill it with clean, warm water and dip your face into it. Blink several times with each dip.

John Wayne in the 1975 film . While a sequel of any sort was highly unusual for Duke, reprising the role of the "one-eyed fat man" seemed a wise decision at the time. Upon winning his long-awaited Academy Award for Best Actor for his role as the cantankerous U.S. Marshal Rooster Cogburn in (1969), the legend joked, "If I'd have known that, I would've put that patch on 35 years earlier." The two films made Rooster's eye patch such an iconic part of John Wayne's legacy that the wardrobe piece sold for nearly $48,000 at an auction in 2011.

HOW TO **MAKE** CRUTCHES

F YOU'RE THE TYPE of person who's confident enough to head out into the wild on their own, you might also be the type to try and tough it out when you're hurt. Just remember, pride comes before the fall—particularly when you have a leg injury. Whether you're dealing with a sprained ankle, a broken foot or a pulled muscle in your leg, you'll need to take the weight off that limb so you don't make the injury worse. Fortunately, the wilderness provides plenty of materials to craft crutches.

You will need:
- 2 sturdy, forked branches, about 4 feet long each
- Extra clothing, duct tape or any soft material (to be used as padding)

1. Your height will determine the size of the branches you need. If you're a person of average height, crutches made from branches that are 4 feet long will usually sit just right. If you're on the taller or shorter side, adjust the length of your crutches accordingly.

2. Branches with a wider fork work best because they provide more room for your armpit to sit comfortably and you can pack them with more padding. A rolled shirt works well for padding, and you can also simply wrap several layers of duct tape around the fork to create padding. You can also do a combination of both to secure the clothing and create more comfort.

3. While you may find it easier or more comfortable to walk with two crutches, there's always the chance that

John Wayne and Robert Mitchum in the 1967 Howard Hawks film *El Dorado*.

resources may be scarce. If the injury isn't too severe and you can put some occasional weight on the corresponding foot, you may be able to get by with just one crutch.

4. When standing with your armpits resting in the padding, your hands should grip the crutches at the level of your waist with your elbows bent at about a 30 degree angle. To walk, put the weight through your hands rather than your armpits. Move the crutches forward first, then your injured leg forward, then your strong leg.

ABOUT THE AUTHORS

 ILLY JENSEN is the CEO of Captive Audience Prevention Training and Recovery Team. He grew up in the Rocky Mountains and was a Boy Scout, Civil Air Patrol Cadet and avid fan of John Wayne. Duke's movie *The Green Berets* (1968) motivated Jensen to become an Army Special Forces NCO (Green Beret) with multiple tours in Iraq and Afghanistan. Jensen is a graduate of US Army Combat Medic School, US Army Cavalry Scout School, US Army Special Forces School, SERE School, Jungle Warfare School and Anti Terrorism Instructor School. As a civilian, Jensen is a Krav Maga Practitioner and an ASHI Level 6 medical response instructor who regularly teaches wilderness first aid, wilderness survival, orienteering and anti-kidnapping and hostage survival.

 HECK FREEDMAN is the COO of Captive Audience Prevention Training and Recovery Team. She is a graduate of SERE School and has implemented her survival skills in more than 20 countries, covering six different environments, including mountain, arctic, desert, jungle, urban and water. Freedman has been a survival instructor since 2013, and is a rappel master, ski instructor, technical scuba diver, bush pilot, self-defense instructor, Level 6 ASHI Emergency Medical Response Instructor and a Civil Air Patrol Search and Rescue Ground Team Leader.

Jensen and Freedman are also the co-authors of *Survival Ready: Life-Saving Skills and Expert Advice for Surviving Any Threat at Any Time.*

ABOUT
CAPTIVE AUDIENCE

F YOU OR your organization are planning on traveling overseas for the purposes of rendering humanitarian aid to any population in need, Captive Audience: Prevention, Training and Recovery Team can offer training at a variety of levels to maximize your chances for success while minimizing your exposure. Our training courses and services offer multiple tiers including pre-deployment readiness, crisis planning and response and post-incident help.

Some of our offerings include:

- Survival on air, land or sea
- Urban survival
- Desert survival
- Mountain survival
- Jungle survival
- Arctic survival
- Water survival
- Basic navigation

- Advanced navigation
- Personal protection
- Third-party protection
- Risk assessments
- Improvised weapons
- Found object fighting

- Mindset
- Combatives
- Restraint escape
- Evasion
- Surviving captivity
- Self-rescue
- Surveillance detection

If you would like to learn more about Captive Audience or are interested in participating in one of our courses, please visit our website: *captiveaudienceptrt.com.*

Media Lab Books
For inquiries, call 646-838-6637

Copyright 2021 Topix Media Lab

Published by Topix Media Lab
14 Wall Street, Suite 4B
New York, NY 10005

Manufactured in Singapore

ISBN-13: 978-1-948174-82-4
ISBN-10: 1-948174-82-0

CEO Tony Romando

Vice President & Publisher Phil Sexton
Senior Vice President of Sales & New Markets Tom Mifsud
Vice President of Retail Sales & Logistics Linda Greenblatt
Chief Financial Officer Vandana Patel
Manufacturing Director Nancy Puskuldjian
Financial Analyst Matthew Quinn
Digital Marketing & Strategy Manager Elyse Gregov

Chief Content Officer Jeff Ashworth
Director of Editorial Operations Courtney Kerrigan
Creative Director Steven Charny
Photo Director Dave Weiss
Executive Editor Tim Baker

Content Editor Juliana Sharaf
Art Director Susan Dazzo
Senior Editor Trevor Courneen
Designer Kelsey Payne
Copy Editor & Fact Checker Tara Sherman

JOHN WAYNE
ENTERPRISES